# The Ahqulieah Chronicles

## The Flight of the Eagle

# Ahqulieah

### Meaning 'Eagle'

Louise A Langley

# The Ahqulieah Chronicles

## The Flight of the Eagle

Ether Publishing

First edition published 2009
by Ether Publishing Ltd

**ETHER**
PUBLISHING

A Voice of Inspiration Publication
www.thevoiceofinspiration.com

ISBN 978-1-906437-02-2

Copyright © 2009 Louise A Langley
Louise Langley's website address is
www. louiselangley.com

A CIP catalogue record of this book is available
from the British Library

Louise Langley asserts the moral right to be identified
as the author of this work.

All rights reserved. No part of this publication may be
reproduced, stored in or introduced into a retrieval system,
or transmitted in any form, or by any means, electronic,
mechanical, photocopy, recording or otherwise, without
the prior written permission of the publisher.

Printed and bound in Great Britain by
Clays Ltd, St Ives plc.

**FSC**
Mixed Sources
Product group from well-managed
forests and other controlled sources
Cert no. SGS - COC - 2061
www.fsc.org
© 1996 Forest Stewardship Council

## *Qualia*

You cannot truly know something
Until
You have experienced it
Yourself

And yet
It is only the experience
That is
The Truth

For Dimitri

and

The Magus

# The Ahqulieah Chronicles

## The Flight of the Eagle

# *Prologue*

How could she ever have known that there would come a moment across time and space when all that had been, and ever could be, the grace and majesty and radiant beauty of all that she was would be the very essence of the return to love, the return to sacred union?

Her journey, her return to sacred union would, quite literally, become the journey of the one.

She could never have guessed the extraordinary depths of the astounding love story that was to be hers,

to be theirs,

Ahqulieah and the Magus.

# England

*June 2008*

"**W**ho am I?" Louise whispered.

As she stepped into the entrance of the tiny cave, the view so reminiscent of something tugging deep within her consciousness, her entire body began to tremble. The entrance belied the spectacle that lay before her now. The clear quartz crystal walls and ceiling bore witness to a tunnel rising high above her head, a tunnel which seemed to journey to infinity far beyond that which the eye could discern, the mind could conceive.

As she gazed in wonder and began her ascent, rising through the depths of the narrow tunnel, her clothes fell away to be replaced by long white robes. Exhilarated, she felt the pain of the points of the crystal walls tearing at the palms of her outstretched hands as she climbed more quickly. Yet this pain was at once accompanied by the exquisite pleasure of the wonder of the journey. On and on the tunnel stretched, until at last she reached the summit and stepped out into a second crystal cave of equal size and spectacle. She could barely open her eyes wide enough to glimpse the stunning scene before her now in the glare of the shaft of light piercing her vision. As she gazed upon the blue of azure seas beyond the cave's entrance, she felt the very essence of the truth of all time fill her knowing.

And yet, it was not the view, but the beautiful woman who stood before her now that utterly captivated her. Who was this amazing beauty, so full of grace and presence, majestic and radiant, who smiled at her? This smile tore at her heart.

"Who are you?" Louise asked, even though somewhere deep within her she already knew the answer.

The woman's answer, a dulcet lilt upon its delivery, told her what she couldn't quite believe.

"I am you, I am Ahqulieah. I stand before you now, the high priestess of the Pleiades, and yet every part of me is you, beautiful girl. Why can you not see your beauty, your grace? You must now truly understand that only in embracing the amazing beauty of who and what you are, only in truly loving all of you, can others come to love themselves. For in you will be their mirror, just as Adrian was your mirror. As I stand before you now, I tell you that we bring our journey from this Pleiadean matrix of life to the human matrix of life. You know this my darling girl, you are writing about it. This is our plan, the plan of the one, remember?"

As she heard these words Louise wondered how she could ever embrace beauty such as this . . . how could she have the right to be the beauty before her. And yet she understood so well that it was merely the ego, the personality that pushed the truth far from her. In that moment Louise felt her heart infused with the truth and knowledge she had so readily refused to accept for so long now.

Tears coursed down her face as now, standing behind this beautiful woman, stood the man she knew so well, the man who had come to her in her dreams, had held her and whispered to her and loved her. His long dark hair falling across his face, his beautiful knowing smile caressing his lips as his eyes bore deep into her soul. He smiled at her with such love, as he witnessed the deep acknowledgement within her, the knowing that her search was over. He stepped toward her, brushed the hair from her face and whispered,

"No longer do you need to look for me. It is now time to stop, as only then will it be possible for me to find you."

An unspoken bond passed between them, a deep remembrance, and she knew he was coming for her.

As she gazed upon his beautiful face, the power of his majesty, his grace, radiating about him, she knew beyond all doubt that he was with her now in the human matrix, playing the game of life. All she needed do was continue to play the game, allow her heart to guide her, allow the events to unfold and he would find her.

She understood that it was only when she could finally embrace the amazing grace, beauty and majesty that were her, that she truly deserved the love of this man. No grief filled her heart now. No notion of being separate or torn apart from this man, but rather a sense of deep joy and peace, and the knowing beyond any doubt of his determination to find her.

It was with this deep sense of peace that she stepped back into the tunnel, long dark hair whipping about her and white robes tearing against the crystal walls in her descent; the love of the ages etched upon her face.

# Crete

*July – August 2008*

As she stepped off the plane and onto the Cretan soil once more, Louise was anticipating spending a relaxing holiday with her three boys. The balmy air of the midsummer sun flushed against her face and caressed her senses, as the gentle breeze tugged her long hair from its clips. How she had yearned to be in Crete; traversing the heights of Spinalonga Island, drinking and laughing with friends, bathing in the extraordinary and healing energy of the little fishing village, Plaka.

For here was her healing . . . always.

How could she possibly have anticipated that the love of the ages was waiting for her now . . . here . . . in Crete?

So many events were unfolding around her in their usual rollercoaster style fashion. It seemed that as every day passed, she came closer to whom she knew her man to be and yet, still, he had not presented himself to her. She was beginning to understand that every man she had met since that extraordinary moment when she had met Adrian in Dublin some two years ago, was part of an exquisite journey . . . a journey to remember the truth of love. Her heart jumped as it remembered the moment of their meeting. Never had she had an experience such as that . . .

never had he. They had both known instantly that the love they shared in those few moments in Dublin was a love that had always been between them. As he had held her, whispered to her and touched her, their tears had mingled with their words as they had expressed their incredulous knowing of having spent life times upon life times together. In those moments she had touched the sacred truth.

As the ensuing months passed and her journey began to unfold, she trusted that this was all part of the universal design to bring her together with the man who had held her so often in her dreams, a presence she found so challenging to articulate to others around her. She trusted in the perfect moment to bring them back across many lifetimes to sacred union.

This was a love that so many around her still struggled to understand. How could she be so in love with a man she had yet to meet in this reality, whom, for so many, there was no proof that he even existed?

How could she trust so deeply that he would find her?

How could she be so sure that the universe would bring them together?

It was simple.

She knew there was only one rule and that was to follow her heart, implicitly, without hesitation, without question, no matter how crazy it seemed.

And . . . trust . . . in perfection.

For each of the men she had met on the trail which was leading her to him, to their union, had brought a deeper understanding and embracing of the love of herself.

She had been in awe and wonder as the heady heights and wretched depths of all that she had experienced over the past two years since meeting Adrian, had taken hold of every moment, every essence of her heart.

From that time, as she touched the sacred truth with Adrian, she was no longer Louise. This she knew with all her soul.

It seemed as if the people she had known before meeting him were strangers to her now, distant as if characters in a film she was watching.

She had not understood who she was and yet she searched.

She had become a child, led by the hand and held by the universe in the most extraordinary fashion, as she continued to follow the trail of synchronicities and synergies, codes and clues that became her journey.

And what a journey it had been. A journey that was to see her leave behind everyone and everything as the search for the truth became her entire purpose for being.

Whilst in Antarctica three months before, Louise decided to take note of the signs and changed her middle name to Ahqulieah, meaning eagle. The eagle, she knew, was the bringer of hindsight and foresight, the messenger of the gods. The energy that this name carried was all that she knew she needed to assist her in carrying out her purpose, completing her journey . . . and yet . . . she had not been prepared for the moment when she would truly know the amazing grace and beauty and truth of who Ahqulieah was.

And so, as that moment had come upon her, she had wept in awe and wonder at the beauty who claimed to be her.

It was as she understood that she and Ahqulieah were one, that they were destined to bring their union, their love of the ages to this, the human matrix, that she finally understood her own worth. She knew that she now deserved the love of this man, and he her, and so, with this knowing . . . she had arrived in Crete.

Sitting under the stars in the garden of the little bohemian café run by her dear friend Stefi, Louise sat chatting and laughing with her friends, watching her children dance to the vibrant sounds of the local band playing Greek music. She could hardly believe that this was only her second night here. Time seemed always to take on a new form when she was here in this little village.

"Ella agape," Stefi called out from behind her and Louise turned to look at her friend. Head turned and deep in conversation, caressed by the gentle evening breeze, something made her momentarily glance back around.

As her vision drew her to a tall, slim, bohemian looking man strolling in through the garden gate and up to the band, her jaw fell open. It was as if time stood still.

Speechless, she watched the man talking animatedly to his friends playing in the band as he struggled to fasten a wayward strand of his long wavy hair from falling across his bearded face.

"Stefi," she called urgently, "who is that man?" Stefi watched her friend's expression with interest.

"Which man?" she asked, a smile spreading rapidly across her beautiful face.

As Louise turned back toward the band to point him out, he was gone.

"He just came in. Tall, slim, very bohemian

looking, long wavy hair, bearded, three quarter length shorts and t shirt . . . he is gone!"

"It could be Dimitri. Why your urgency to know?" Stefi gently teased her friend; she could sense her shock.

"Because," Louise barely whispered in her state of shock, "he is the image of Adrian from Dublin!"

As she strode down onto Driros beach, laden with beach bags falling off her shoulders, Louise laughed as she called out to her friends Emma and Michelle to help her.

The boys were stripping off under the olive trees at the base of the newly built beach bar, hot and clearly intent upon leaping into the sea immediately.

Louise dropped her bags on the sun beds, searched in her wallet for some coins and headed straight toward the beach bar to buy them all some water.

"What a relief," she thought, "that this year the hotel had changed hands, and the new owners had decided to not only extend and refurbish the existing hotel but also build a beach bar."

Her thoughts strayed lazily toward the man she had seen fleetingly in Stefi's café just two nights ago. How shocked she had been as she had been faced with the image of Adrian. Could it be that the universe intended to send him to her now in yet another form?

"I guess if it's meant to be, he'll just show up again out of the blue," she thought to herself as she ordered her water and began chatting in Greek with Juli, the woman who was serving behind the bar.

She had the sense of someone watching her. She

turned to her right and sitting on a bar stool, hair protected from the sun by a large straw hat, was him. His face broke into a knowing grin as their eyes met, his stunning blue grey eyes piercing her very being. She felt her heart smile as it bathed in his presence for those moments.

They chatted idly in Greek about the hotel, the fact that he was originally from Athens and that he was here temporarily to complete contract plumbing work for the hotel.
 As she listened to his very deep melodic voice, she struggled in places to comprehend his strong accent. Hearing the children calling, she said goodbye and strolled back down to the beach, leaving him gazing after her and grinning broadly.
 "Did you get his name, did you exchange any details?" her friends asked her.
 Just as she was explaining that she hadn't, Stefi arrived with her son Jiannis. Stefi once again studied her friend's animated face as she confirmed that this man was indeed Dimitri.

Since the summer of 2006, directly after Louise's chance meeting with Adrian, Stefi had watched her change. She emanated a radiance which dazzled many of the locals as they strived to understand what had caused this huge shift in her.
 "Go speak to him again," Stefi encouraged her friend, but as they turned back toward the beach bar, he had vanished.
 "What was the universe up to?" Louise thought as she smiled deeply at the synchronicity which had just brought them together for a second time.

It didn't take long to find out.

The sun was beginning to dip in the late afternoon sky and Michelle, Emma and the kids were hungry. Louise seemed to have lost her appetite all together!

As Emma was heading out to the airport and home to England that night, they decided that they would eat at a local taverna which overlooked the stony beach of Plaka. No sooner had they settled themselves at a table, joined by another friend Jess, than Emma leant forward to Louise and declared,

"I don't believe it. Guess who is sitting behind us?"

Louise glanced along the stone promenade, to see Dimitri sitting with two of his friends, just a few tables away. She watched him throw his head back in laughter at something one of his friends had said to him, his eyes vibrant and alive and the golden flecks in his unruly dark sun bleached hair glinting in the light of the dipping sun.

His head turned toward her and his cheeks flushed as he caught sight of her. She too felt her face flush as an incredible feeling swelled within her heart, infusing her entire being. They began to steal glances at each other, only when they thought the other wasn't watching.

After some minutes had passed, he stood up from the table and strode into the ocean. He swam out into the sea, brushing his hair from his bearded face as he watched her from the distance, amongst the waves. Her boys laughed, watching their mum spellbound by this man, as they remarked upon his striking resemblance to the figure of Jesus. She continued to steal glances at him for the time he remained in the ocean until he returned to his friends at the table.

Settling the bill, Louise began to walk back along the promenade after the others who had headed on towards the car. As she passed the table where Dimitri still sat, she glanced down toward him. He smiled up at her and they began to chat.

"Sit with me," he murmured. Every part of his being was stirring as he watched this woman that so entranced him, standing before him now. How was it that she so affected him in this way?

"I cannot now, I have to leave to take my friend to the airport," she replied, faltering in her Greek as her heart leapt.

"When can I see you then?" he responded instantly.

And so they agreed to meet the following night in The Pine Tree, Stefi's café, at 10 pm.

She stood on her balcony much later that night with her friend Georgina who had arrived that evening. They gazed upward together toward the full moon and stars above them, seeming as if they were almost within their reach. Was it her imagination or did the stars seem to be winking at her tonight?

# The Ahqulieah Chronicles

As Georgina and Michelle headed off to bed, Louise sat alone on her balcony high above the village for many hours, deep in union with the cosmic display before her. She loved gazing at the stars and here in Crete, above Spinalonga Island, the cosmos always seemed to appear in its most spectacular form.

She thought of her experience connecting with the beauty of Ahqulieah in meditation just before she had left England. She remembered her man's words to her during that meditation as he had spoken so softly, imploring her not to search for him . . . and she thought of Dimitri and how he so resembled Adrian.

What magic was in their meeting? And then she glanced up to notice a shooting star dart across the dark of the night . . . and she smiled.

Taking a pen, she began to write under the stars.

She wrote at speed to keep up with all that flooded through her consciousness in those moments:

> *How may the ocean speak to me, till I have ears to hear?*
> *The wind whisper her secrets, till I do call her near,*
> *The sun caress my cheek so fair and call me to my home,*
> *Until the moment I stand still, remember all once known.*
>
> *For glorious are the days so sure that I do hold within,*
> *The very mention of their name, the miracles they bring,*

*The journey laid out here to tread that they
   do show me sure,*
*Are just a moment's calling, when I listen
   once more.*

*"What is love?" I hear you ask, I feel you
   search so deep,*
*May I touch it, feel it here, as heart begins to
   leap?*
*For only in its knowing sure may miracles
   unfold,*
*And ages past now, evermore, may once more
   be retold.*

*How the moon does smile so well, caress me
   with her thoughts,*
*And cosmos bring the secrets true of evidence
   now caught.*
*The signs so sure are here again and wisdom
   set out here,*
*So head may once again take heed and heart
   be ever near.*

As she lay in bed, she wondered at the meaning of the words she had written.

"Are you sure you said ten o'clock?" Stefi teased her friend the following evening as they sat at a little table outside The Pine Tree drinking a beer together in the warm evening breeze.

Louise nearly choked on her drink as she chuckled and told of her inability to remember anything clearly that she and Dimitri had said to one another the previous day, such was her state of enchantment at that time.

"I'm sure I said ten. I have no idea if I definitely said Saturday," she replied.

For all her light heartedness, something was tugging deep at her consciousness, the same something that had left her so shocked in the first moment she had seen him.

She had sensed in that moment an energy which emanated from this man, an energy she had encountered only once before ... in Dublin. Yes she had met men similar to the image of Adrian, however, not carrying this energy. There was an inexplicable energetic thread which seemed to be pulling them toward each other. Could this be the thread that pulls soul mates together? Would this be something she would be able to see?

No sooner had this thought entered her mind than Dimitri strolled around the corner of the café and headed toward where she and Stefi were sitting.

It was as if her question had been answered

instantly. For as she looked at him she noticed that an incredible aura of white and golden light shrouded him, energy which seemed to appear as magical dust, dancing around him in the dark of the night.

A smile instantly broke across his beautiful face as he saw her and sat down in the chair opposite her as Stefi jumped to her feet to fetch him a beer.

Time seemed to stand still from that moment. It was as if everyone and everything disappeared from their world as they spoke at length, exploring so much about each other. They laughed as she consulted her Greek/English dictionary for words she was striving to articulate in Greek as he didn't know any English.

After some hours they left the café and drove together up the majestic mountain which bordered Plaka and the ocean, to a place where they could sit and watch the stars. As he drew her closer to him, listening to her explain the ancient Egyptians' understanding, ceremony and ritual around the cosmos, he knew that the only desire that consumed him was to reach out and touch this beautiful woman. Who was she really? What had conspired to bring them together? What were the white golden dust particles of energy that he could see dancing around her? She was so very different to him and yet in his heart they felt so very much the same; part of the same one.

"It is as if your energy and my energy come together to create a new third energy," he explained to her as he took her face in his hands.

"When I am with you, I feel light and as a child once more," he continued. The expression etched across his face as he asked if he may kiss her was one she would never forget. This expression was one of absolute trust in the face of total bewilderment as an inexplicable force drew them so close.

"I know you," he whispered.

"I know you too," she replied as tears slowly fell across her cheek, shooting stars darting high above them.

As they strolled beside the ocean in the dark of the night, along a tiny track which was edged by an old stone wall, she couldn't quite believe that this was already their third night together.

As they stopped he urged her to sit on the wall beside him. They gazed out to sea and then skyward at the stunning stellar display above them. The moon carved out a path of light which glimmered magically across the gentle waves as if the very essence of the alchemy of all time were contained in that jewelled path.

He looked deep into her eyes as they talked at length. The balmy air enveloped their senses and he lay down, his head in her lap as she gently stroked his hair from his face. Their smiles completely mirrored the love they felt for each other in those moments, their eyes alive and vibrant with what seemed to be the love of the ages.

He began to tell her how he loved her. How he had loved her from the first moment he had seen her.

"It is erotas," he explained, instant love, very different from lust. He continued to describe how her energy had captivated him. He felt like a child, light in her presence, and once again he spoke of their two energies becoming one together. She knew that he spoke the truth, for this is how she too had felt from the first moment, utterly captivated, as if there were nothing but them.

# The Ahqulieah Chronicles

He began to ask her about sex, what she understood to be the sexual union. It was challenging to speak with her limited Greek vocabulary, to explain what she knew to be the sacred sexual union and so they began to talk about energy.

Something pierced her heart, saddened her, as she began to describe that for her, sex was a union of two people, of their hearts, their energy, their physicality becoming one and that sex could only and would only be this. The sacred union.

Why did she feel such heaviness in her heart as she spoke those words? A vision, a deep remembrance, swept through her with such force in that moment.

She was standing somewhere far from this reality, within another lifetime, high upon a podium of stone, wild wind whipping about her, the train of her long white robe billowing behind her.

The early evening sun caressed her cheek and carved out an incredible golden path stretching far below her toward distant white shores. She touched her finger, sensing the markings on the ring set on her slender finger, feeling the power of its alchemy. This ring bore the pledge of their sacred union, their oath to find each other always across time and space. It was as if the very touch of that ring called him to her, for instantly, she felt his breath upon her cheek, his presence behind her and the familiar electricity that passed between them as they experienced their oneness.

His hand reached out to gently pull her face toward him, refractions of sunlight catching his identical ring and his knowing smile spread across his beautiful face as his long dark hair fell from behind his ear to obscure his vision. She felt utter bliss as he whispered to her, knowing what would now come to pass.

They walked together hand in hand from the podium to an opening in a meadowed glade. They were quite alone. The sun held them in its embrace as they lay together naked, these two luminous beings with white golden dust particles dancing about them as they touched divine love in their union . . .

"I cannot just give myself to a man only for the pleasure of sex. For me, it must be a complete union," Louise said with a gentle voice as she gazed at Dimitri, the anger and irritation at her words appearing across his troubled face, clearly visible under the light of the moon.

How could she not see the love he felt for her? Had he not told her already how instant that love had been? How could she not see that he, a man, wanted her, a beautiful woman, with all his heart?
There was no logic behind the way he felt for her, what he saw in her, around her. He just knew.

He spoke with angry passion as he explained that he too felt like this, that he was not a man who would choose to have casual sex and was surprised that she could have thought him so. If that were the case then she really didn't know him at all.

As they drove home together, silent and deep within their own thoughts, she noted how something had shifted so deeply within her in those moments of remembrance of that other lifetime, and now quite evidently within him too.

Dimitri was beautiful; his energy had captivated her from the outset. She knew that this was no coincidental meeting. It had certainly been divinely orchestrated and, with all her heart, she knew that she would love him to take her home and explore that sacred sexual union.

Why had her head stepped in, begun to reason in a crazy illogical manner, the moment she had recalled that moment from another lifetime? Why had she become so sad, so detached from this man before her in that moment as if nothing could replace or compare to the union that had gone before?

This had been the first time since she had met him, she realised, and that she had moved from the joy of her heart into her head. How many times had she advocated to everyone around her that the only way to truly experience your amazing journey of life and witness its miracles unfold around you, was to implicitly trust and stay in your heart always.

She had strayed and, as she looked at the expression on the face of the man she adored sitting next to her, she knew the moment had gone . . .

Some days passed before she saw him again. When they met again, the expression upon his face made her heart sing as he sighed deeply at the sight of her. How much he had missed her, he noticed.
    Sitting together under the stars they spoke of the many things that intrigued them both. He loved listening to her speak in her simple Greek. He told her of his deepest desire to visit Edinburgh castle.
    "My castle," he called it.

They lay together in a passionate embrace for many hours, both looking forward to the time when they would be alone together in the little house on the beach she had decided to rent to extend her stay here in Plaka.

Her heart was urging her to stay now, instead of heading back to set out on the writing trail around Celtic Britain as originally planned. She remembered the magical experience the last time she had stayed in this little house and wondered if this was where the universe intended her and Dimitri to consummate their union.

Later, as he left her at her gate, kissing her and telling her he would see her the next day, she watched him climb into his car, a broad smile across his face and that golden white aura dancing about him.

As she stood on her balcony, gazing towards the Milky Way which was clearly visible amongst so many stars in the dark of the night, she heard the distant hum of the little fishing boats setting out to sea for the next day's catch.

She considered that, for a man who could travel anywhere in the world, how coincidental that he was so drawn to Edinburgh. How she would love to explore his connection to the castle with him.

Fleetingly, she recalled the moment that she too had so desired to be in that castle, to stand in its uppermost turret. A force so great had drawn her there and held her in its embrace as she had undergone her first initiation. This, she now understood, had been the true beginning of her journey, the moment she had placed that ring upon her finger.

What did the castle hold in store for Dimitri?

The following week passed without them seeing each other as his work kept him up all through each night. Every time he spoke to her, she could hear the tiredness in his voice. Every day he said he hoped to see her the following evening. He continually apologised for the huge problem he was dealing with as the plumber of this newly opened hotel, explaining he was having just one hour's sleep each night.

By the Friday, she was ready to move into the little house by the sea. Kissing and hugging her boys as she left them with their father who had just arrived, she set off to the little house and began to unpack.
 "Ella agape, my baby," Dimitri said joyfully as she picked up the phone at 9.30 that evening.
 "I am just finishing work and am coming to this beautiful house and to my beautiful baby. I will be with you within the hour."

Later that night as she lay in bed, basking in the energy of this amazing house, her heart was heavy. Why had he not arrived? Why had he not called? Why had he not picked up when she had called him? They had waited all week to see each other and he had sounded so happy to be coming. Why did she deserve this? Why did this man treat her in this way?
 She knew oh so well, as she told all those around

her always, that everything is perfect. Somewhere in the craziness of this was perfection for her, but she could not see it. Her heart was torn apart and she lay, so numbed, feeling that the universe had dropped her from a great height.

She barely slept and the following morning, there was no word from him at all. She spoke to Juli at the beach bar and explained what had happened and Juli was shocked. This was not the behaviour of the Dimitri she knew and she was worried that something had happened to him. She insisted Louise ring him to check he was okay. He did not pick up the call once again.

And so, bewildered, Louise set off for Spinalonga Island, to climb the mound to the summit. As she boarded the boat to Plaka, her heart yearned to reach the summit of that island, knowing the healing that awaited her.

She scaled the heights of the island and then noticed Dimitri had been trying to call her. The island seemed to whisper to her as the wind whipped wildly about her, sun streaming across her face.

As she closed her eyes, she was infused with majesty and strength, a calm descended upon her and she called him back. He was so happy to speak to her, apologising for not coming the previous night.

"I ran out of hot water, was unable to bath and, exhausted, fell asleep while I was waiting for the water to heat" he explained. Now he was keen to see her.

What was she to do? Berate him for not contacting her? The poor man had been exhausted, this she knew. She also knew that it was her own perception that had questioned his desire to be with her, not his.

Later that day, when she called him as promised, she spoke her truth to him. She explained that when he did not call or show up she had felt he did not want to see her. He was shocked and explained that this was absolutely not the case. That evening he arrived exactly at the time they had agreed and apologised again for the night before.

They spent an exquisite evening together, talking at length, eating, laughing and then finally coming to lay on the bed in the little bedroom of her stunning house, looking out through the window to the stars that gazed upon them in all their magnificence.

As they kissed, and their embrace became more passionate, she felt deep within her that something was missing. Why was it that, after so much energy that had passed between them, she now felt detached?

Louise felt a sense of relief wash over her as Dimitri's phone rang. The call was expected and it was his signal to return to work in Iraklion. He promised to call her and come to see her if he returned before 4 am. He did not.

It was two days before they saw each other again. Exhausted, he laid his head in her lap on her sofa and they chatted. A connection so huge, an inexplicable attraction was so evident for them both.

He gazed at her, wondering what she truly saw

in him. She looked at him, feeling so blessed to have found this man. He carried such an extraordinary energy that he clearly wasn't aware of himself.

"Will you come to Spinalonga Island with me?" she whispered to him.

He smiled "Yes, I will."

Two days later as Louise waited for Dimitri by the boat that was to take them to Spinalonga Island she chatted to the locals about her writings. They were so interested in all that she spoke of and listened with eager anticipation.

She had a deep sense that the island was calling Dimitri, yearning to infuse him with the energy that was so clearly Atlantean; pure, light and vibrant. For the island was surely the doorway to so many dimensions; she had felt it from the first moment she had stepped foot there those two years ago after meeting Adrian.

What would it unlock in him, in both of them today?

He arrived, rushing from work to be with her. Her heart yearned to reach out and hold him, to heal him when she saw him. He looked so tired and under pressure.

No man had ever engendered in her such a yearning to be the woman, to nurture, to heal, to love and to be all that she could be to serve him in every way that a woman can love a man.

They sat quietly on the boat, hand in hand, the wind blowing wildly about them as they crossed the sea to the island.

Striding up the side of the island, they didn't

stop until they reached the mound at the top. Laughing together in the wind, his phone rang and she watched him walk away from her, angrily speaking to the person calling him back to work.

In those moments, she silently called out to the island to heal him as he walked, to heal this man who carried such energy that he could not see himself. The gentility and strength of the Christ consciousness coursed through his entire being and yet he seemed completely oblivious to this.

They strode across the top of the island, he taking her to places she had never seen before. As they reached the far end, they came upon a stunning scene. As she stepped foot into the centre of a ruined stone walled circular structure, it seemed as if this resembled the structure of a building from a distant memory, a building with stone pillars, gauze wafting gently in the breeze, standing high upon the world looking down upon distant shores.

Dimitri took her hand and led her to a single archway set out in the stone wall. As she stood in the archway, touched the stone of the wall and took in the magnificent view of distant shores and azure seas so far below, tears fell down her cheek. For she remembered in those moments, all that it was to be the priestess, all that the glorious state of bliss, of mastery of energy, of complete oneness with the universe always had and always would be.

As surely as she remembered that union with the universe, so she remembered the extra-ordinary depths of love, of union, of oneness with her sacred partner. The priest and the priestess.

As Dimitri steadied her on the precipice as the winds blew around them, she turned to look at him and knew that he felt some deep knowing tugging at his consciousness. His eyes were alive and vibrant, radiating a light she had not seen in them before.

Still holding her hand, he led her to a steep craggy descent, just below the stone circle, and they sat. She knew instinctively that this was the place and the moment to give him healing. As she began, the elements gathered their strength.

She called out to the universe, asking for all the energy that had ever passed between them both to be brought into great balance.

It seemed as if every dimension responded in that moment through the wind which suddenly grew so wild that, had they been standing still, they would likely have been blown off the edge of the precipice.

She felt the love of the ages utterly infuse her as the strength of the energy that passed through her to this man astonished her.

Suddenly the sky was dark, moonlit in fact, and the birds she could hear soaring above them were eagles. A gentle stream of water rippled from a nearby stream and his breath caressed her cheek while he sat, eyes closed and legs about her.

"Heal me Louli," he laughed gently as she fell back into his arms.

"How amazing to be back here with you, once more," she murmured, realising she had quite clearly stepped into another lifetime, another reality.

"You are always with me," he smiled at her now. "Weave your wonderful magic. Heal me please."

She stood up, walked around him and knelt behind him. As she gently placed her hands on his shoulders, she began to softly sing the words that so effortlessly flowed through her.

"Remember I told you once, if you ever find me in another lifetime and I don't remember, find a way to help me," he whispered.

"I remember," she replied through her song. "I will."

"Promise?"

"I promise" she laughed gently.

It was brilliant sunshine and, as she drew the healing to a close and opened her eyes, the look in Dimitri's eyes was one she would never forget. For etched across his face, in his eyes, was the expression and truth of all she had felt in those moments, the love of the ages. He gently kissed her and they began their descent, laughing so as they struggled to stay upright in the torrent of wind gusting about them.

Could he have experienced the same thing as her?

When they reached the bottom of the mound they sat drinking together at a café, overlooking the sea awaiting their boat to take them back to Plaka village. Dimitri was so calm and relaxed.

When his phone rang demanding he came back to work, he spoke in soft dulcet tones reassuringly.

They let one boat pass and took the next, sitting in a state of bliss and oneness at the bow of the boat, hand in hand, with no need for words.

Louise felt a deep sense of peace as he left knowing that, he had recovered some sense of who he was; the amazing beauty and strength that was him, across all time.

The feeling in her heart was growing in intensity moment by moment as she longed to care for this man.

That night, a night they had intended to spend together, passed with him working and by the time the following evening came her heart was heavy, for she knew that they had just a few days left to be together. Louise could not understand why they had not had the opportunity to be together more, why the universe had orchestrated it in this manner.

By the time she spoke to him she was numb. He explained he had a problem with his car and asked her to please come get him. It was clear from the moment he sat in her car that he was exhausted once more. He had no appetite and only wanted to stay at home. They sat and talked for hours about many things, as they tried to understand what was happening between them.

It was clear as he spoke that he had questions around their union; how it could work between them with her living in another country, having children and travelling with her work?

That night, as they lay together, he had no energy to make love, only to hold her. And in the morning as he woke to go to work, she began to question herself. Did he not think her beautiful? Did he not still feel the erotas they spoke of, why had he not made love to her? Why had he questioned her about so much? Didn't he feel worthy enough to be with her? How could he not see what she saw in him? Could he not see his beauty? Could he not see that she loved him for who he was now?

As these questions plagued her mind, a great

battle was occurring within her, the battle of the head with the heart.

And it hurt . . .

"Come to a Cuban bar in Iraklion with me now."
It was 8.30 pm and Louise was sitting in Stefi's garden, chatting.

"I thought you said you wouldn't see him tonight," Stefi laughed. "You are tired."

Louise grinned. She was tired, but the thought of seeing him made her feel alive again. And so she went.

As they arrived, Louise was introduced to his friends and they all headed for the bar. There it was again, the strange feeling of detachment. What was it that was creating this between them?

In the salsa bar he asked her to dance for him, refusing to dance with her as she gazed at him incredulously. Why would he not dance with her? She felt distinctly uncomfortable.

She stepped outside where she felt an instant relief wash over her and returned a call to a friend. Why was she behaving this way? She adored this man. Why did she feel so uncomfortable? Was she uncomfortable with him or was she really uncomfortable with herself?

Dimitri came out twice to look for her and each time she was still talking.

As she stepped back into the bar, she could tell from the look upon his face that things had completely changed between them.

As they drove home together he was angry and there was very little communication between them.

She tried to explain, but she knew that what had happened between them this night had been beyond explanation.

Why had she not told him the reason why she felt so uncomfortable? It had been as if she was determined to sabotage this relationship ... but why?

Two days passed with no communication between them as neither of them called the other.

Her heart was heavy as she headed for Spinalonga Island, yearning to envelop herself in the healing energy of that island. As she retraced their steps, traversing across the top of the island, her heart was torn apart.

Every step she had taken with him was to her as if the dimensions had opened and their union had bound them in those moments across all realities, across time and space.

As she reached the end of the island, the place where he had teased her so, standing in the centre of the tall stone walled circle, she gazed out through the majestic ruined archway which seemed to hold the vision of all things, all places, all realities.

High above the world, she gazed through that archway to the blue seas and white shores below, as if looking down upon all of humanity and her heart wept and rejoiced in that same moment.

She took from her bag a little stone she had bought, the crystal that held within it the shape of aleph; the structure of life within a leaf, and she placed it in the centre of the ruined circle.

As she did so, she called out to the universe, cried

out with the full force of her soul, for all the love that ever had been and ever would be theirs to be bound by the healing energy of this beautiful island.

As she climbed down the side of the hill, the way marked only by the steep descent of the ruined stones beneath her feet, she came upon an old ruined church, by the side of a well.

She sat here for some time, sat within the arch of the bleached stone wall; sun streaming upon her face, warming her senses as her heart defiantly presented the truth of their love to her over and over again. A truth which defied all physical evidence in those precise moments and yet, she knew it to be true.

She was so weak.

She called upon the strength of Ahqulieah, of the universe to help her to come to a place of understanding.

She could not understand why she had felt so uncomfortable that evening in the Cuban bar . . . and yet she had.

And, as the sun so gently caressed her, a soft breeze brushing her hair from her face, a deep understanding flooded her consciousness.

She had been uncomfortable with herself.

He had shown her the love he always had . . . in his way.

She had at some level felt unworthy to be with him.

Felt as if she was not able to please him in the way others could.

Tears began to fall down her face, for how was she now to explain this to him? How would he feel if he understood she had felt this unworthiness?

Would she ever have the opportunity to explain?

**W**ould she ever have the opportunity to tell him? He was leaving Crete for a holiday in Cuba on the same day as she was travelling back to England.

And so she decided to write him a letter and leave it with Juli at the beach bar.

> Dimitri,
>
> I am writing to you because I want you to understand what is in my heart.
>
> From the moment we met, the moment I saw you, I had a deep love in my heart. This love is a love I have only felt once before, in Dublin, two years ago.
>
> It was then that I began my journey, a quest to understand who I truly am.
>
> So much has happened since then, much which has had me follow a trail like a child – held by the universe. Much which I wish I could have spoken to you about, which has had so many around me astounded as they have watched my story unfold.

*I did not expect to meet you. It has been a true blessing. I feel as if we are one and this I know you have felt too.*

*It is because I love you that I want you to have the life that you choose, one that is perfect and full of love and honour for you as this is what you truly deserve. You are a beautiful person and have taught me so much, more than you could possibly know.*

*If you choose that you wish to spend more time with me, that you feel in your heart as I do, then I would love that.*

*If you choose to allow your journey to unfold without me then that is perfect too. As long as you are happy so am I.*

*I hope that all is fabulous for you in Cuba.*

*Kisses,*
*Louise*

The early morning sun streamed through the shuttered window of her bedroom. It warmed her senses and touched her heart.

Her heart was alive; full of joy and vibrancy once more, for, in writing the letter she had spoken her truth and found herself once again. She thought of Ahqulieah and she remembered the promise of life and love.

Smiling and laughing, she rose from her bed. As she glanced in the mirror her smile broadened, for there in front of her was the radiant beauty once more, the childlike essence she had when she arrived in Crete . . .

How young she looked now and how full of awe and wonder at what she seemed to know was to unfold today.

She pondered now, how once more she found herself letting a man go that she loved unconditionally.

"But who can truly let anyone go," she thought. "For possession, control and ownership are illusions. The only control is that within. Everything that I am, all that I have experienced has happened because I have created it that way. The question is what do I choose to create now?"

She stared into the reflection in the mirror as she considered this deeply, "I choose to see his gentility and love for me once more. Not to own it, possess it or control it. Just to witness it in its purest and lightest state . . . as it was in the beginning together when we were both so free to be in our hearts."

The universe heard and the universe delivered, instantly.

As she ventured to the beach, radiating with the extraordinary energy, Juli beamed at her. She declared that she had never seen her look so beautiful.

They began to talk animatedly about all that had occurred, Juli wanting to know whether Dimitri had called after reading the letter the day before. As they chatted and laughed at length, they did not notice at first that Dimitri had arrived at the beach bar with his work colleagues.

He looked across at her, stealing a glance, as Louise raised one hand to acknowledge him and then continued to talk to Juli.

For some time Dimitri worked near them, glancing at her often. She could see how low his energy was, how tired he looked. In those moments she knew that he was remembering, and connecting to the beauty of the energy that had become their oneness.

He was connecting back to his heart.
He could not take his eyes off her.

After some time, she left the beach with her friend Kate, heading back to her little house. They talked about the synchronicity of Dimitri being at the beach in those moments, seeing her radiate with the beauty that she was once more. The universe had surely orchestrated this, preventing him from seeing her over the previous few days until a deep understanding had brought her to this state of peace.

Later that day, they returned to the beach and headed down the steep steps to the side of the water sports area to find her friends George and Angelos. She heard someone calling her and as she glanced back over her shoulder, she saw Dimitri working. She couldn't quite believe it.

After some moments he looked toward her, his entire expression so openly demonstrating his desire for her to show him that she cared.

As she smiled at him, his face broke into the knowing smile she had seen so many times before, and yet this time it captured a vulnerability and complete expression of his love for her.

So obvious was it that those around remarked on it.

For her, those moments were bliss, for they showed her how her truth had been so right, that this love had truly passed between them.

And with all her soul, she thanked the universe for giving her that opportunity to see the love in his eyes and heart for her once again. She had no idea whether he would call her now, in one week, one month or five years. No idea whether their journey was to pan out together. What she did know was that all would be perfect, whatever perfect meant for them both.

That evening as she wrote, she really had no idea what the universe was about to create now ... and yet there was one thing she felt she was really beginning to understand. Every part of being alive was the beauty of growing. That was the reason for life.

As she sat on the beach with Stefi in the early hours of the morning, the moon carving the most dramatic path across the ocean before them, the only sound was that of the waves lapping against the large stone boulders of the beach. As she gazed up at the stars . . . the stars smiled back at her.

"As above, so below," she whispered into the balmy night.

As the day dawned, she awoke in a state of wonder at what the journey would bring today.

Sitting under the pine trees on the beach, laughing and talking with Kate and George, she began to feel deep resistance within her to trust and allow the universe to complete the story in the way it was designed to be completed. Why was she feeling this way?

She must trust.

Her ego was screaming at her to control the outcome, to know what lay ahead, and yet, how could the miracle of your story of life be that miraculous journey of excitement, of experience, of intrigue and of miracles, if all that lay ahead were already known?

Tomorrow, she realised would be the full moon, exactly one month since she had first met Dimitri.

"Ah, the synchronicity of cycles, beginnings and endings," she thought.

As she fell asleep, knowing that tomorrow was her last day in Crete, she knew what she would truly choose the promise of the full moon to bring, without attachment ... just one more moment together.

Louise and Juli sat together at The Pine Tree the next evening, drinking an early evening coffee. Juli had been so busy at work all summer, and this was the first opportunity they had had to really relax and chat at length together. They gazed toward Spinalonga Island watching the spectacular full moon rise into the sky. She was breathtaking, deep orange in her hue.

As Louise dropped Juli back into her little hometown of Elounda some hours later, Juli suddenly asked Louise to pull the car over.

"Dimitri is there, Louise, sitting in the tavern. Go and speak to him," she urged her.

He was shocked to see her, believing she had already left. He explained he had friends from Athens joining him for dinner, and asked her to join them.

They talked into the night, each sharing their story and Louise enchanted them by telling them of her journey of discovery.

It was strange, Louise felt Dimitri was distant and yet not in the same moment. When she explained to him that she had written an entire book surrounding their unfolding love story, the final chapter still not yet complete, he asked her to tell his friends about it, smiling at her with a glimpse of the love that he felt so deeply for her.

As they finished eating, he took his friends off to find their new holiday accommodation saying he would try to see her later.

It was already very late. How many times had she heard that and he hadn't called?

Why would he call tonight?

Maybe because . . . tonight was the full moon . . . and she had asked for the chance for a moment together.

At midnight, as she sat on the beach with Stefi and gazed at the full moon eclipse, she realised that the universe had already worked its magic.
They had had their moment.

He didn't call.

Somehow, she had known that he wouldn't.

And yet,
What is sacred love if not unconditional?

She loved him as he was, unconditionally, trusting in his need for space to find the love of him.

She was leaving and a deep sadness and a sickness filled her heart. She had experienced so much with Dimitri, so much of the heady heights and wretched depths of love.

She headed off for one last trip to the beach. As she sat under the shade of the pine tree talking to Kate, they spoke of how Dimitri needed his space and time now, in Cuba. How they both needed their space and time.
   Louise was heading to Ireland the next day and she sighed as she thought of the healing energy that Ireland always brought to her.

Now, as she and Kate spoke of how things always seem to break around you in order for the path forward to become clear of all distractions, Louise explained her shock when she had read the headline internet news that morning.

Hurricane expected in Cuba within three days . . . the day he would arrive.

 Just as she spoke these words, a loud noise in the sea before them shook them to the core. For the windscreen in Angelo's speedboat had shattered completely.
   She and Kate looked at each other in shock. What greater confirmation could she possibly need than

that of how things are broken around you in order for you to see the clear path ahead?

Later, after she had said her goodbyes to her many friends, she set off to return to her little house.

The pain within her grew as she approached this sanctuary that had been hers for that short while. Her heart was breaking, stretched beyond all limits.

For in the very moment that she opened the door and entered, she felt utterly dejected. She could scream with the pain that coursed through her now, the pain of all that had been, all that could have been, the love so deeply entrenched throughout her entire being and the incredible sense of loss of this man.

And, as her body began to convulse, her senses screaming, she fell to her knees unable to see anything but the unhappiness before her eyes.

As her music played, she gazed at her bedroom, the white mosquito net so beautifully tied and hanging above the wooden bed that Dimitri had so admired.

She felt so betrayed in that moment, for they had never made love . . . everything had conspired to make it so.

Why? In this, the most romantic little house upon the sea, in one of the most dramatic and stunning settings in the world.

She could hardly breathe now as her tears fell and yet, somewhere, deep within her, she knew that she had taken an immense magical step forward in her journey of life; in understanding the truth of love.

This feeling was exquisite in that moment.

And then the phone began to ring.

It was Stefi, "Louise, come and have a drink with me before you leave. I have come back from The Pine Tree so I can see you."

As she sat drinking tea with her dear friend, both were at a loss for words as they considered what had unfolded over these past few weeks.

Stefi had been so happy at the thought of Louise and Dimitri coming together. She had felt a deep sense of honour and uniqueness within Dimitri which she knew was so befitting of the love her friend deserved.

Now, she was deep in wonder at what may be the path ahead for them both.

Only the universe knew . . .

## Dublin, Ireland

*August 2008*

"Ah, home," Louise sighed, the moment her feet touched the streets of Dublin. What was it with the energy of Ireland that always made her feel so vibrant and yet so totally grounded and at one with the earth? It was as if her very soul became alive, with a determination to unearth the truth in all things when she was here. Her heart lifted instantaneously and she felt the promise of her journey return. Here was to be her healing.

How many incredible, catalytic life changing events had occurred for her here in Ireland, events which had forged her life's journey?

Checking into Trinity College in Central Dublin, she dropped her bags into her room and headed straight to the Central Library and The Book of Kells Exhibition, this book being the oldest Celtic book in existence.

As she walked through the halls directly to where The Book of Kells was housed under its glass case, she glanced toward the eagle displayed upon the wall, the word "Aquila" boldly written beneath it. The eagle was one of four key symbols beautifully illustrated within the book and depicted in its Latin name "Aquila".

"I still haven't changed my name by deed poll," she murmured, as she took out her notebook and began to write a reminder to herself.

As she did so, she fleetingly noticed a marking next to the eagle on an opened page in The Book of Kells. This mark was the same as the one that she had seen this summer on the page of the Gospel of St John, which was on display in the little church on Spinalonga Island. It had caught her eye then, predominately because of its likeness to Ogham script, the ancient Celtic script she knew she had found in so many places, so many writings, paintings and codes. This Ogham script was amazingly linking together so many stories across time, legends, mythologies, mysterious characters with no facts to substantiate their existence, and yet, with phenomenal evidence within so many ancient texts and scripts to substantiate their links and their purpose.

Strolling through the great library within the college, she yearned to climb the ladders to the uppermost shelves of the old bookcases. It was as if the books were calling out to her to come and hear all the secrets that they had ever set out to tell those who would listen.

She thought about those authors who had written the messages within these books, those who, like her, were so passionate for others to feel the excitement, intensity and delight of the unfolding stories within their pages.

Louise realised that everybody has the most amazing story to tell, the story of their truth, their journey and their mysteries. For there is no greater story than that of the energy of truth, passion and experience, the stories that encourage the reader to be set out on their own adventure and take that free fall dive into the abyss of the unknown and the vulnerability of the heart.

Later that evening, she sat chatting at the bar at one of her favourite places in Dublin, The Café en Seine.
"Where in the world could you be so happy, so loved for who you truly are and be surrounded by those who love life, than Ireland?" she smiled to herself as she ate and drank.
She chatted to so many who hopped onto the bar stools next to her to join in with the laughter and chatter. She thought of Dimitri, of her love for him. Maybe one day, she could bring Dimitri here . . . one day when they had found peace in their union . . . one day when they were friends once more.

"You know, these markings are the same as those found in Glastonbury Abbey, supposed burial place of King Arthur," Louise explained as the tour guide standing within The Fourknocks burial chamber explained the relevance of the Neolithic markings above each of its four chambers.

She had decided to hop on a tiny tour bus the following day. It was taking a route to the sites she had always wanted to visit and she considered that it may be fun to join a few strangers en route, "after all you never know who you may meet," she thought to herself.

The tour guide smiled at her.

"Do you know much about the origins of these markings, their links to Ogham script, and the tales of Irish mythology which state their purpose?" he asked her in his beautiful southern Irish accent.

"It really is the most attractive accent in the entire world," she thought to herself as she smiled broadly. She could just sit and listen to this man all day!

"I would love to hear more," she replied eagerly. "I know that the markings are also identical to some found in ancient Egypt, on the walls of some of the buildings and chambers that have been forbidden entry now.

I know that evidence showing that Egypt is much older than has been claimed, is in existence but, is generally kept from the public in order to ensure that certain religious books are not compromised in their facts.

I know that pyramids, particularly step pyramids, are now being found all around the world including Europe and that the links between the ancient civilisations of Egypt and Neolithic Britain and Europe are clear.

I also know that the symbology contained in the centre of this symbol is identical to that at the centre of some of the key Mayan symbols," she went on, "and that Ogham has been found in paintings by Nicolas Poussin, the artist whose paintings are closely associated with Rennes-le-Château in France, and Bérenger Jacques Saunière, grandmaster of The Priory of Sion. He was supposedly the priest of Rennes-le-Château, encoding intriguing symbology into the structure of his church, the Magdalene Church, to set out the notion that life is a game. The Poussin paintings he hung there have Ogham script within them via poses and gesticulations of the muses portrayed on the canvases. These codes deduce a particular spot on the Val-Dieu, a spot leading to secrets of Jesus, of Mary Magdalene.

I know that Ogham script was used by the druids to create great alchemy, that it is comprised of merely lines and dots, something that forms the basis of many of the original sacred languages recorded on the planet. I have found a very common thread running through the ancient Irish tales, which links the stories of some of the key mystical characters of the ages, those such as King Arthur and Jesus. Throughout these tales, Ogham script is present. In fact, all stories or characters, whichever word you wish to use to describe them, throughout the ages globally seem to have their roots in the original Irish mythology," she concluded.

The tour guide threw back his head and laughed so.
"Well, well young miss," he laughed. "It seems I have an assistant for the tour."
She laughed with him and he began to explore with her the most incredible tales, some she had never heard of, those which had been handed down in generations of families, never quite reaching the pages of a book.
"You know," she went on as another member of the tour, an Italian man called Walter, joined in with their conversations, deeply interested in what she had to say. "I have a theory I would love to share with you."
"Go on," the guide encouraged her.
"What if Atlantis was never a single place, but many places, including Ireland? What if Atlantis was a word used to describe a state of being, a way of living? What if this Atlantean way of living was an energetic state of being where we were able to use our telekinetic abilities to communicate, to create, travel, learn and love? A new level of human consciousness. What if that was what the huge change of 2012, so explored and debated, is all about – a return to that state of living, of being. Of course, 2012 could be out by up to 40 years according to the Mayan elders as their calendar is cyclical and the Gregorian calendar, by which we calculate time, is linear," she went on.

# The Ahqulieah Chronicles

Both Walter and the guide were listening intently now.

"I had the amazing privilege to visit Antarctica earlier this year," she continued, "and just before I left, I found out about a Jesuit priest who, in the 1960's, discovered an ancient Egyptian map depicting the island of Atlantis. With 20th century satellite imaging, it has been revealed that the land mass beneath Antarctica is identical to the land mass on the map found by the priest. Geologists have also now determined that Antarctica used to be sub tropical, totally aligned to the state of Atlantis. Just two days after we left, a huge ice mass broke away from an area we had been sailing around, proving that the area is warming now. The thing is," she went on, "I have found evidence for so many places on the globe being identical to maps of Atlantis that have surfaced over the ages. Great philosophers and writers such as Plato and Aristotle have written about Atlantis and its whereabouts, all in very different places. Anyway, that's my theory," she concluded.

"I like your theory very much," said the guide, smiling.

Walter jumped onto the little minibus next to her as they headed toward the next spot on their journey and they began to speak at length. She spoke of all that had occurred between Dimitri and her over the summer and of her deep sadness at the manner in which they had left one another.

Walter began to recite to her a poem he had written. By the time he had finished, tears were streaming down her face.

"That is wonderful. You have a great gift," she murmured, smiling through her tears.

"You know, sometimes the love we desire is right in front of our face and we just can't see it," he said. "We can't see it because we won't see it, because it is a dangerous place to be. Sometimes, that love presents itself to us in ways that we could not imagine and, because we are taken by surprise, we instantly surrender to it. It is only after we surrender to it that we begin to feel the danger in it. This man must have been so deeply in love with you. If he were not, he wouldn't have concerned himself with its future," he continued. "I know what it is to love someone deeply and be fearful of being so vulnerable in my heart," he spoke gently in his beautiful Italian accent.

As the day went on, Louise and Walter had great fun together as they visited ancient monastic buildings, Neolithic burial chambers and scaled the heights of the stunning remains of derelict sacred buildings.

"Where else in the world could you possibly have free reign to climb ancient sacred buildings such as these, without restraint and in total isolation," Louise thought to herself.

Their final destination was Tara, the stone of destiny set at the top of a labyrinthal mound at the seat of the great Irish kings of old. It was said that all the truth of your heart could be made manifest at this stone of destiny, the truth of your reason for being here.

They laughed so much, for the moment they

approached Tara and prepared for the very exposed walk to reach the stone, torrential rain and wild wind whipped up about them.

It was impossible to stand upright in the face of the torrent of wind and, as Louise reached out and touched the stone, her heart full of delight, she cried out to the elements.

Laughing, she declared that the wild elements were absolute conviction of the transformation happening within her as her voice faded amongst the roaring of the storm about her.

Soaked, but warmed from a mug of hot chocolate they had shared together in the little cafe at Tara, Walter and Louise climbed back onto the tour bus to head back to Dublin.

As she told him of her name change to become Louise Ahqulieah, he explained that the eagle was the standard bearer of St John, the so called favourite disciple of Jesus. He continued that in fact, it was St John who Leonardo Da Vinci had used to really depict Mary Magdalene in his famous, and now much debated, The Last Supper painting.

They spoke of the many scriptures and theologies around the globe, the common threads that seemed to appear between them all. For he, just as she, had dedicated himself to exploring the true meaning of these threads. He had experienced so many of the things that she had on her journey, both energetically and physically.

They spoke of the alchemies of Horus practised in ancient Egypt at the Temple of Isis, of the evidence that substantiated this practise. They spoke of why the stories of Jesus and Mary Magdalene had been distorted to hide these facts, to hide the knowledge that the human being can, through the practise of sacred sexual union, transcend in form metaphysically to another state of being.

"Wow," they laughed together. "Imagine the churches deciding to issue a proclamation that only through sexual union are you able to reach a true state of connecting back to your divinity. Imagine them acknowledging the real sacred goddess, the chalice to immortality, to the origins of life, surrendering the power of the male to a force greater than the sum of the male and female, the energy of androgyny."

It was then that she began to tell him of the origins of her third book. As he listened, his jaw fell open in delight.

"Cuba hit by worst hurricanes ever. Hurricane Gustav devastates the capital and many areas of the country."

She read the headline of the newspapers greeting her at Gatwick airport as she stepped off the plane from Dublin.

Without hesitation she called him, but his phone was switched off.

With a great sigh, she knew that she must trust. This was his journey and she was on hers.

# England

*September 2008*

"So, tell me, what has been happening with you over the summer," Louise's dear friend Cherry asked as they sat in her kitchen drinking a mug of tea. This was the second person, since she had returned from Ireland, that Louise had talked of her time with Dimitri.

The first had been with her friend Michelle who had been so eager to hear Louise's news. She had held her friend and wept with her as she remembered seeing Louise and Dimitri together in Crete, remarking once more upon their extraordinary connection, one which had been so evident to all surrounding them as they had watched them together.

"There is no denying his love for you," Michelle had whispered lovingly to her friend, "even a blind man could have seen that love, sensed it with his heart. Every gesture he made with you, the way he looked at you, smiled with you and became a child again with you, was a love so beautiful to watch that it has inspired me to know that this is what I choose for myself. Watching you two together was like watching a beautiful dance unfolding. You were both in complete harmony and rhythm with each other," she had continued.

After talking with her friend further, Louise knew she needed to return to Crete in October. She must go back to complete the cycle that she had left open as she had departed in that tumultuous state of misery. She knew deep within her that, whether she saw him or not, was irrelevant. It was only important that she was there once more. This decision defied logic; this was a decision purely from her heart.

As she began to explain to Cherry what had unfolded in Crete, the tears coursed upon her cheeks. Cherry sat listening, her striking blue eyes glistening with wisdom of the ages as she took in all that Louise had to tell her.

Cherry really had and always had an amazing ability to hold her in a space, very maternally, as she came to understand the threads running deep within her experiences.

Not only was Cherry a practitioner of various forms of very powerful healing, but she was also someone who expertly helped people to access their many past and future lives. Powerful soul regression therapy, as this process was known, was something Cherry had been practising for some ten years now.

By the time Louise had finished talking about the trip to Dublin, the trip she intuitively knew she needed to take, she felt very different, almost cleansed. Matt, Cherry's son and the musician who had written the music to accompany Louise's first book, stepped into the kitchen, hugged Louise and commented on how well she looked.

They chatted for a while, discussing impending plans, until Cherry looked at her and said,

"Right, my dear, are we ready to begin our regression today, ready to see which past lives we may uncover?"

As Louise began to drift slowly toward the earth, like an autumn leaf falling gently in the soft breeze, Cherry's voice faded to a distant murmur.

She had stepped foot within the walled, cobbled streets of an ancient and beautiful castle she knew so well . . . Edinburgh Castle.

The dark of the night was upon the castle and as she glanced about her, Louise saw many druids sitting on the ground in small groups surrounding blazing fires, laughing as the flames flickered and danced daringly in the pitch of the night.

There was a sense of alchemy, expectation and celebration in the air. Young boys wielding barrows and carts were laughing, women adorned in long velvet robes were singing and the druids were chanting something quite inaudible and yet hauntingly beautiful.

Cherry's voice whispered to her from a distant place, "Who are you? What is your name? What are you doing?"

She looked down upon her long simple robe, her long dark hair whipping about her in the gentle breeze of the night as she skipped with delight along the cobbled street which wound its way up within the castle walls. Her heart was so full of joy, so full of love and she basked in a heady state of bliss.

"I am Mautheren. Tonight, I marry the man that I love. I cannot quite believe that he loves me. He is a beautiful man, both a nobleman and simple man. He has such magic within his eyes, alchemy of such magnitude that it exudes from his entire being. He is a Magus and I, a Mage, have been his student for some time now. He holds deep secrets of the universe and people travel from very far afield to hear him speak."

As she spoke these words, she saw him appear in the distance before her, surrounded in a light so white, so bright that it dazzled her.

This light, this electromagnetic field, was formed of moving particles, a magical dust, which danced against the pitch black of the night that surrounded him.

The dust emanated from the crown of his head and reached out to the heavens it seemed, in a shaft of brilliance. From his feet, the dust danced down the cobbled street in the black of the night to reach Mautheren and surround her too.

She raised her arms and threw her head back, laughing, as the dust flowed through her fingertips and fell upon all those that she skipped past sitting around their fires on the old cobbled street. How they laughed with her, a sense of great alchemy and delight spread across their faces.

"My students," she noted as she watched the children's joy as they received the dust.

She came to stand before the Magus, the love now alive and dancing through the core of her being. Never had she known a moment such as this, where the universe seemed to sing so loud, when her heart was singing the song of the universe to her. The song of truth; the truth of the alchemy of love.

How blessed she felt to be binding herself in union to this man she thought, as she looked upon his beautiful face, so vibrant and alive, the love he felt for her etched across its every detail.

As the light of the dust and the fires about them flickered and created shadows across them both, he stretched out his hand to touch her face, his long dark hair falling across his lightly bearded face and his stunning blue eyes bearing deep into her soul. His eyes were timeless, ageless, and full of the long held secrets of the universe.

"Do you recognise him in this life time?" she heard a faint whisper echo from somewhere distant. Her heart responded outside of the realms of logic.

"Dimitri" she murmured. And yet something was different . . . his love for her . . . his strength emanating through the very essence of him, as if the very power and control of the universe was totally at his fingertips.

As she gazed in wonder upon this man she loved so, she felt as if her very self stood before her. All were delightedly running toward them now, the people of the castle, showering them with tiny red rosebuds.

A robed and hooded, tall and slender dark figure quite suddenly loomed behind her Magus, James. The figure emerged from the dark of the night sky to beckon James to listen.

As the figure began to speak, the words which slipped effortlessly from his mouth pierced the heart of the man before her, of James, as the understanding of the oath he had taken so long ago, now took hold.

This oath was to give up his most treasured gift in exchange for the knowledge of all things.

"It is time," the figure spoke gently, "time to leave this reality. Your mission here is complete."

Still clutching her hand, she felt his body falter as he implored her with his tear filled eyes to understand what he had done.

She, a mage, his mage, understood how easy it could be to pledge anything in exchange for the pursuit and understanding of the knowledge of all things.

She felt the energy of the figure behind him caress him with tenderness, understanding and love for a man such as he.

Her heart reached out to James, through her every essence, as she spoke the words he was so evidently shocked and yet at once enraptured to hear.

"I will go with him . . . he will not go alone."

The dark figure looked upon her beautiful tear stained face, the face that bore the mark of the unconditional love of the ages, and spoke with such compassion, as if determined to find an honourable manner in which to facilitate this passage.

"There is only one way that you may come too and that is for you two to merge and become one being."

As the enormity of his words began to sink in, she heard a distant whisper, "Is this Azrael?"

Mautheren had no idea who Azrael was. She understood only that this figure was most clearly determined to find a way to allow them to be together.

James begged her with his eyes, his heart, the tears coursing upon his face now.

"I cannot ask you to do this to be with me," he whispered.

"You do not ask me," she smiled and spoke gently through her tears. "I offer myself to you in union always. I am your Mage and you my Magus. Our union is sacred and we have spent so many days and ways making it so. It is my honour to become one with you for you are to me all that is life and love."

"Tonight is the night of our union," James murmured, turning to face the dark figure.
"Allow us please to consummate our union first and then we will willingly fulfil our oaths."

The dark figure smiled, his face alive with a great unworldly radiance.

"My children, look about you at these children that run in the cobbled streets far below where you stand now. Know that they, and their children, and their children's children, will always tell the great story of unconditional love where the two offered themselves as one to be forever more united. This story will be written into a book that passes through the ages, and through this book all will remember the druid magic. Your work here is complete and it is time for you to merge. You may spend this night together and understand that it is the very act of your consummation that will begin the merging of you two into one being."

As he watched the tears streaming now across James' face, he murmured, "You will have many more chances to be together in human form. Go now and begin your consummation and meet me in the turret before dawn."

A shaft of brilliant light, magical illuminated dust, seemed to explode around them, holding these two in its alchemical arms. James, still clutching her hand tightly, led her up the steep and narrow spiral staircase to the regal chamber which lay in the northernmost turret. From the window they watched the cosmos dance for them, beckoning them home.

He laid her gently on the bed and began to make love to her, the beauty and love of the ages that he had sought for so long and had now finally found.

They both wept as the ecstasy of the union they experienced now took hold of their entire being. It became so sacred and they shook uncontrollably in its grip. They climaxed somewhere so high within their heads and then seemed to leave their bodies altogether and bask in the bliss of these moments in another place, another universe.

Never could she remember a moment such as this . . . and yet she knew that this was and always would be their union, their love of the ages . . . and knew that this was not new to her experience.

They heard a distant chanting whispering through the wind and knew the time had come to climb to the uppermost turret, to fulfil their oath.

As they stood out on the exposed summit of the turret, the wild wind whipping about them as they wrapped their arms tightly around each other, the dark figure spoke to them now in an urgent and yet at once, loving and reassuring tone.

"It is time now."

James looked deep into her eyes and she felt his breath upon her cheek for the last time as he held her so close to him and whispered, "Our hearts will become one. You know this my darling. You know what the knowledge has shown us. It is because our hearts will become one once more that we will always know each other, in every reality, dimension and existence."

She reached up to touch his face and, in those final moments as she saw the love in his eyes and in his smile, they quite literally began to merge into one being.

She heard him urgently whisper to her, "I will never forget you. Wherever you are, I will find you. I will know you the instant I lay my eyes and heart upon you once more."

Although she heard his words, she no longer saw him in front of her. She was now within him, one being, and as one being they climbed together a stairway of light, of magical dust in the sky that had emerged before them.

As they took the final step from dark into light, a deep sense of understanding and bliss flooded their knowing. They smiled as they sat at a large desk, gazing upon a huge leather bound book, debating which story within this game called life they would play out next . . .

"You are coming back now," she heard the familiar voice whispering to her from the distance, "back to my room Louise."

As she began to come back to the present, Louise, her heart still utterly infused with the love of her sacred union, a voice from another dimension was urgently pleading with her to, "Follow the trail of the rose." She was being bombarded with information that she must not forget; places, facts and mysteries across time and space that would be expanded upon soon.

Cherry looked lovingly down upon her tear stained face and wiped the hair from her eyes.
"Wow. That was quite a journey. I think it's time we had a cup of tea, don't you?"

Could it be that only two weeks had passed since she was last sitting in Cherry's kitchen, Louise thought as she wondered what would unfold today. Her intuition had urgently pleaded with her to explore another journey with Cherry so, here she was.

Cherry led Louise into her room and instructed her to lie on the bed.

"Before we start today," she began, "there is something I must tell you. It was when you last left me that I suddenly remembered something, something to do with your ring from Edinburgh Castle."

Louise instinctively touched the silver, blue incised ring on her middle finger, sensing its energy.

"Louise, remember that it was when you were standing in the uppermost turret of Edinburgh Castle in December of 2005 that you had that sudden recollection of another lifetime?" Cherry continued.

Louise remembered all too well. She recalled the intense feelings within her as, stepping into another lifetime and standing before the promontory in that turret, she waited for something, for someone.

"Remember that it was as you walked back down the stairs of the turret in a trance-like state, stunned at what had just occurred, that you walked into the little shop at the base and purchased your ring; the ring that truly began your journey?"

Yes, Louise would never forget that moment. She had had no desire to purchase any jewellery as she didn't really wear jewellery. And yet something about that ring had utterly captivated her. She knew deep within her that she had no choice but to purchase the ring, wear it immediately, and not take it off.

It was a long time after that time, after meeting Adrian in Dublin, that she came to understand the significance of this ring to her, the significance of the message incised upon it in Ogham script, the message that read 'blessing on the soul of L'. In fact, it had been Cherry who had instigated her intense period of investigation into the true origins of the ring, the source of its message and the alchemy surrounding its intent.

Cherry took a deep breath.
"Louise, think about it, you were standing in the uppermost turret of Edinburgh Castle when you stepped into that other lifetime. The very same place where you and your Magus, who seemed so like Dimitri, merged to become one."

How could she not have realised this before? She was stunned. Once again she remembered that deep sense of waiting for someone, something, as she had stood looking out upon the fields of Edinburgh from that turret in her trance-like state.

Silently tears trickled down her face as she recalled how her journey had unfolded from that moment. Her quest was coming full circle, her quest for the truth of her story, her search for the truth of her love. Who was the man she had merged with in Edinburgh Castle? Who was he truly? She knew now that the answer to this question was the answer to her quest.

"Lie back and relax now and let's see where we find ourselves today," Cherry whispered to her gently.

Once more Louise found herself drifting gently to the earth on what seemed to have become a very familiar journey to her now . . . and yet each time she ventured into the next journey her heart was at once engulfed in the only truth of the life set out before her.

It was late afternoon as she felt the soft dewy grass beneath her bare feet as she strode across a steep green hillside. The dipping sun caressed her cheek, warmed the back of her long simple white sack cloth robe as the breeze gently loosened the threads of the silk rope tied about her waist and cuffs.

A small gothic castle stood behind her, the points of the many turrets reaching high toward the darkening sky as the smoke from many fires surrounding the castle hung upon the late afternoon mist. These fires were alive, vibrant, alchemical and full of expectation.

Her long dark hair, tied to the side in a plait which reached her waist, outlined her slender frame, pale face and large dark eyes . . . the eyes of an alchemist.

All about her were druids and alchemists, tending the fires which were giving birth to great alchemy. Rainbow coloured dust particles rose from the elixirs bubbling over these fires and seemed to trickle in a constant stream from their vessels down and along deep trenches carved out through the ground, until they met a moat surrounding the castle. The rainbow particles of dust continued to rise high above the castle as the alchemical liquids ran down through a gulley in the moat to a little hut on the edge of the forest.

The hut was tiny, flanked by leather skin walls and a roof thatched with an unusual binding of straw and twigs.

She gazed toward the hut, luminous against the darkening skies. A deep sense of knowing, expectation and exhilaration flooded her senses at the thought of meeting its resident for the first time today. For the man who occupied this quirky abode bore such a reputation. Known as the Magus it was his role to instruct, observe and oversee the alchemical processes carried out by the many druids and alchemists about her on this hillside, all of whom had been under his instruction for some time now.

But not she. This would be her first visit to him and she had been told that she must prepare something quite extraordinary in order that he may speak with her and take her under his instruction as a mage.

A whisper in the breeze, a magical voice urged her to begin a descent down to the base of a steep and craggy cliff which bordered the hillside. This voice seemed so familiar to her, the voice of the universe, the voice of home, as it directed her through the wild torrent of wind whipping against her body as she climbed down to the foot of the cliff.

The voice grew more urgent as it instructed her to find a specific tree, a tree with a twisted white trunk that would appear barely alive.

She laughed in the wild wind as she caught sight of the tree, conspiring with the elements to help her stand in an upright position in the stead of the torrent growing about her now.

"Find the red berries that appear as red stone, deep at the base of the roots," the voice whispered.

As she reached down to the base of the tree trunk, her hand effortlessly slipped through the earth opening a chasm before her. There, to her astonishment, was a cluster of the most beautiful, tiny, uncut red ten sided crystals, the shape of dodecahedrons.

"Take seven," the voice continued, "And lay them in the shape of the symbol. You remember what to do."

With seven clasped in her hand, she climbed back up the side of the cliff, the wind easing as she reached the top.

With the remnants of the dipping sun once more warming her senses, she instinctively began to lay out the crystals upon the dewy grass beneath her feet to create a six pointed star.

In the centre she carved out a simple cross, the sign of the Vesica Piscis and of the ether. She took leaves she had collected from the tree and placed one leaf in each point of the six pointed star structure, encoding aleph into the symbol. She knew of the power of the alchemy of aleph, the sacred geometric structure contained within a leaf.

She strode over to the moat, scooped up a little of the bubbling liquid, poured it into the centre of her symbol and watched as the entire symbol merged before her eyes to become one stone.

The appearance of the stone was not particularly special, hardly noticeable except for the unmistakable glow that emanated from it, the glow that displayed the promise of alchemy. It felt cool to her touch as she clasped it tightly within her hand and strode over to the hut, sitting outside its walls awaiting her turn to be seen by the Magus.

The dark and cold of the night drew in as she waited for many hours. With a blanket of cloth wrapped about her shoulders to keep out the cold, she sat for those hours listening to his deep voice as he spoke to those within the hut. She was entranced by the familiarity of his dulcet tones.

With her eyes closed and head resting upon the walls she began to sing softly to herself, until she heard him laughing gently with her, his presence overwhelming her.

She opened her eyes and gazed at his face illuminated in the moonlight. As he leant down toward her he extended his hand to gently help her to her feet.

"I have waited for many ages for you to come; to return and show me what you remember," he murmured as he led her deftly into the little hut.

He took his seat behind an old carved wooden table opposite her, an enormous white eagle sitting reverently behind him.

His startling blue eyes bore deep into her as

he brushed a strand of his hair from his cheek, revealing more of his lightly bearded face.

"What have you brought me Luli?" he inquired, a mischievous glint in his eye.

Slowly, she took the stone from her hand and placed it gently on the table before him. He raised his hand and held it over the stone, head bent and eyes fixed upon its form as it began to change before them.

An incredibly haunting music quite suddenly filled the entire hut, the space about them glowing vibrantly now in the hue of the stone, the hue of the little crystals she had found beneath the tree. She could feel the incredible vibration of alchemy of the greatest form as it saturated the air about them. The eagle flew toward her and sat nestled in her lap as the Magus raised his head to smile upon her, his eyes filled with tears.

"You have remembered!" He caressed her with his words, his hand reaching hers and pulling her to her feet as he motioned for her to come with him now.

She stood in wonder as a portal, a stargate, appeared before them in the wall of the hut, opening into a very long white crystal tunnel, its sides dancing against the dark of the night as if made of moving magical particles.

Holding her hand gently in his, he began to lead her through the tunnel toward the point of darkness in the distance. She felt at once both dwarfed and yet uplifted in the presence of this extraordinarily powerful man.

The darkness came upon them as they stepped

through the end of the tunnel, a darkness which was spectacularly lit by a sky full of constellations she had never seen before.

They stepped toward the edge of a great chasm. He held her very steady in the wake of the gentle breeze as she gasped at what she saw before her now. For thousands of metres below and centred in the chasm, was a four sided precision-made rectangular stone tower.

The tower changed colour continually as it emanated light waves of alchemy, dancing through the dark of the night.

As the Magus whispered to her, "Do you remember Luli, it's so important that you remember what we built, remember that I have been waiting for you, waiting to bring you here again?" she fell to her knees.

All around the edge of this vast chasm, an entire city of stone was materialising before their very eyes. In just moments, it was far greater than a city; it was a whole new world reaching beyond comprehension.

The sky was illuminated now with particles of light and dust and it seemed as if all before them that had appeared solid was not.

The Magus turned to her now, pulled her to her feet and looked deep into her eyes with great compassion as he saw her wrestling with remembrance.

"Who are you really?" she whispered, hardly able to talk.

"You know who I am," he replied, smiling at

her. "I am many names to you Luli, many names across the notion of time and space . . . Ben, James, the Magus. Have I not been coming to you, to your dreams for some time now, waking you gently, and loving you, whispering for you to remember Luli? It is time now to remember. Take my hand and walk into the void with me."

There was not one element of doubt within her as she clasped his hand and stepped over the edge and out into the great void of chasm before her now. She knew deep within her, that with this man by her side, everything was possible.

As they came closer to the centre, the light waves of alchemy emanating from the tower began to whip into a torrent of wind, a tornado reaching from the tip of the tower up and far into the heavens.

"Are you truly ready to be with me, to trust me no matter what? If not we can turn back now," he called out to her, his voice rising to be heard against the noise of the wild torrent before them now.

For a moment he transformed before her eyes into a great beast like creature, poised, determined to give her every reason to be full of distrust for him and change her mind.

Louise heard the faint and familiar voice of Cherry urgently beckoning her, "What's happening?"

"He wants me to have the chance to distrust him, and yet with every essence of my being I love this man and would trust him with my last breath."Louise murmured.

She smiled at him, as the wild wind lashed her

hair across her face. Instantly he took the form of the beautiful man once more as he held her hand so tightly now and led her directly into the torrent ahead.

Disoriented in the midst of its power, they began to witness all that they had ever been together flash before them, as if watching scenes from films. The wind was drawing them in an ever decreasing downward spiral toward the tip of the stone pillar below. It was as if the breath of creation was pulling them home now.

She barely heard his voice in the midst of the wind about her as he urged her to understand that they were to merge into one being together once more. The thought of this filled her with a deep sense of knowing, remembrance and love.

Quite suddenly the noise abated to silence as they drifted down through the top of the structure into the centre of a spectacular white crystal temple.
With their feet firmly rooted on the surprisingly welcome icy floor beneath them, they gazed at the beauty of the many tunnels of crystal leading away from the central chamber. A shaft of brilliant light appeared before them now, whispering to them to move toward the altar before them.
As they neared the crystal altar, they looked down upon a huge ancient leather bound book laid open for them to peruse. The shaft of light was beginning to take form as it urged them to prepare to merge as one being. Light was flooding through their bodies now, down through the palms of their

hands and dancing out through their fingertips as codes of creation leaping magically into the pages of the book before them.

As they watched the pages before them absorb the codes, they suddenly found themselves being pulled into the book and into complete darkness.

"Where are we?" she whispered, feeling him with her still.

"Open your eyes and see," she heard him gently say, laughter evident within his voice.

She was astonished to find that they were standing back on the edge of the forest, the little hut behind them and the cold of the night brushing their cheeks once more.

As the Magus took a leather strap from his belt and gently bound their two wrists together he gazed down upon her astonished face.

"This journey was only possible because of the stone you made Luli," he smiled.

"What would you choose now my darling girl?" he whispered as he gazed upon the face of the girl he loved beyond measure, the girl he knew to be far more powerful than she could possibly conceive.

"To be bound to you, to be by your side and to create alchemy together for all time," she smiled.

His face was alive and vibrant with his love for her as he stood before the crowd of alchemists who had gathered before them now, dancing and celebrating at their union as he declared for all to hear, "So be it."

They sat beneath the stars together, she between his legs as he enveloped her in his arms, warmed her with the strength of his body and murmured what was to be now. In those moments she came to understand that this was home, their home, this tiny island with its beautiful, quirky and wild landscape, so full of alchemy and promise. He explained to her that they could take many journeys now together to so many different places, times, realities and always return to this plane, this truth.

"For all we ever need is right here," he whispered, "where we sit, under the magnificent stars surrounded by the forests and cliffs that border this magical land, a land where so many codes and keys are hidden within its embrace."

She realised, as they sat together, that they could see the future that had already come to pass. It was then that the mesmerising sound of a young girl's voice captivated her. She gazed across the plain to see a vision of a tiny girl, long dark hair whisked about her pale heart shaped face and startling blue eyes dancing and singing before her.

"Kethrian, our daughter," the Magus said to her as they watched every blade of grass, every flower head, every bird and animal present bend its face and ear toward this beautiful child singing and dancing in the night.

He watched Louise's face, the remembrance of what was to come to pass flooding her senses, and with deep joy in his heart, he knew that his wonderful girl was beginning to come home to him now.

For how many nights had he come to her, held her, whispered to her, loved her while her head screamed that he did not exist and yet her heart knew that he did.

This was the essential journey to remembrance. He knew what it had taken for her to stand by her truth, to declare the validity of the experiences she had encountered with him, to declare her love for a man so many could not comprehend. How could she love a man that did not exist, so many would ask her?

And yet, he knew that this was the only way for her to return to that incredible place of the power and truth of who and what she really was; the incredible state of alchemy in which she truly resided.

"You are coming back to me now, back to this room Louise," she heard Cherry say as the tears of joy fell upon Louise's face.

Shaken, but with an amazing sense of deep grace, Louise opened her tear filled eyes and smiled at Cherry with the love she felt infusing her entire being.

"Time for a cup of tea?" she laughed.

"I think so." laughed Cherry.

# England

10th October 2008

"**W**hy do you need to change your name at exactly ten minutes past ten today?" the lawyer asked Louise as she sat poised with her pen, ready to change her middle name to Ahqulieah.

"Because today is the 10th October 2008 which, in numerological terms, comes back to 10.10.10. This is hugely powerful in its meaning. The Maya believed the number ten was the involution and evolution of life, the beginning and end of all cycles and all of the polarity law of the universe. Ten also represents unity. All things are energy in essence, therefore to declare the energy of my new name at exactly 10 minutes past 10 on 10.10.10 has a huge impact," she explained to the bewildered and yet deeply intrigued man sitting before her now.

"Well, as we have some time to wait before ten minutes past ten, I would love to hear more. I would love to understand how it is that your name carries an energy which becomes an integral part of your journey in life and how changing that name changes your journey instantly," he continued.

And so they chatted for some time, he felt delighted and intrigued, declaring that he would leave the office today researching this further.

The following day she set out in her car to visit her friend, Emma. Whilst momentarily stationary in the car, she was hit by another car at full force.

She couldn't even remember being hit as she sat, stunned, in her driver's seat, the crown of her head wide open as she felt huge amounts of energy pouring into her.

"Aha" she smiled to herself, "Ahqulieah has arrived . . . and just in time before I head back to Crete!"

*Crete*

*October 2008*

Louise and her boys arrived in Crete and headed straight to Stefi's house. It was nearly midnight as the two friends sat there chatting animatedly. As the boys disappeared into another room with Yiannis, Stefi gazed into her friends face and smiled.

"You seem so at peace," she said, "so much happier than you were when you left here just eight weeks ago. In fact, you seem to have completely changed! What has happened?"

So began Louise's recital of the very many things that had happened to her since leaving Crete, many of which are not relayed within the pages of this tale.

As she finished, Stefi looked at her stunned.
"You truly are a saint," she exclaimed.
Louise laughed at her friend's expression.
"How can you love somebody with such depth and understanding, accepting that all that they have done is merely be a mirror for you to see the areas within yourself you have not yet learned to love?" she continued. "You really do deserve the greatest of loves Louise," she said as she threw her arms around her friend and hugged her tightly.

Just as Louise and the boys were leaving the house, she suddenly stopped, looked at her friend and said, "It's really strange Stefi. A creature ran in front of my car in the dark of the night. It stopped, looked up at me and seemed to smile. "

"What creature was it?" Stefi enquired "I'll bet it has a meaning for you, knowing you!"

"A hedgehog." Louise smiled . . .

It was 2 am by the time Louise had settled the children into bed and was able to stand out on her balcony. The night air was balmy with a fresh gentle breeze.

The cosmic display spread across the sky was, as ever, quite spectacular. The moon seemed to smile at her as the stars glistened with the promise of magic.

She sighed deeply as tears gently fell across her cheeks, remembering so deeply within her heart all that had passed between her and Dimitri over the summer.

Stefi had told her that no one had seen Dimitri since Louise had left Crete. They knew he had returned from Cuba, unscathed by the hurricanes which had devastated the entire country, but he had not been seen anywhere near Plaka at all.

She looked skyward and called out to the elements, to the cosmos and to the universe.

"Please give us the opportunity to come to some peace between us, to come to a place of peace in our love for each other, whatever form that love takes."

She knew that she meant this with all her soul. She had no need or attachment to have to spend time with him. Just to see his love for her etched across his face once more, together with his exquisite knowing smile, was all she asked for.

With this feeling lodged deep within her heart, she fell into bed and slept.

The crickets were buzzing, the birds were singing and the sun was streaming in through her balcony doors as she awoke the next morning. She laughed as her boys jumped onto the bed with her, demanding their mum get up immediately to sample the pancakes they had made for breakfast.

They set off in the car some fifty minutes later, singing with delight at the music that was playing. As they rounded the corner of the coastal road and passed the entrance to the hotel where Dimitri had worked all summer, Louise suddenly pulled the car over to the side of the road.

"Please wait here for a moment," she asked her boys as she leapt out of her car and began to walk up the steep drive toward the hotel.

"Could she have really just seen what she thought she had?" she questioned herself.

She was sure she had seen Dimitri's car parked in the drive. As she looked up toward three men, standing with their backs to her, her heart leapt. There was the familiar figure of the man she loved, animatedly discussing details with his colleagues.

Fleetingly, she considered how alike he was to the man she had encountered in another lifetime, another Edinburgh Castle.

Without a moment's hesitation she called out to him "Dimitri!"

Was he dreaming? Did he really just hear her voice? He turned to look down the slope toward the place where the voice had come from. His heart sung as he leapt off the terrace he was standing on and sprinted down the drive toward her, grabbing her and kissing her on both cheeks.

"Ella agape" he said to her in his deep dulcet tones, a beautiful smile spread across his bronzed face. He held her, his hands gently gripping both her arms as he looked deep into her eyes.

"When did you arrive? Where are you staying? Still in the house up on the hill?" he asked, unable to contain his excitement at seeing her.

They began to chat. He told her of his trip to Cuba, the hurricanes. He wanted to know all about the book she was writing, the book which would contain their story.

All the time they were talking, he did not take his hands from her, his eyes from her beautiful face, wanting to reach out and touch the inexplicable energetic thread that was their union.

"Something has changed within him," she noticed as she watched a deep sense of peace speak through his expressions.

Her children began to walk up the path toward their mum, calling out to Dimitri. He smiled at them.

"I only arrived here today for a couple of days and then I must go to the other side of the island, some four hours away. I am working day and night and attending night school, until next spring," he said as he affectionately reached out to hold her face in his hands. "Please call me later today. We can meet."

She smiled, joy filling her heart, and promised to call him later that day as she headed back down the hill with her boys and drove off to meet friends in a town an hour's drive away.

She had asked the universe for a chance for them to come to some place of peace with their love for each other and the universe had instantly obliged!

She knew, as she headed off in the car, that no matter what unfolded now, she had seen in those few moments the truth of his love for her. He had, once again, been so completely in his heart, childlike in essence and so evidently in love with her.

And she loved this man . . . without condition.

Later that day she called him as promised. He picked the phone up directly, excited to hear her voice and explained that something had come up back on the other side of the island. He had to return to attend to it but would be back in Plaka next week, probably Tuesday, for a couple of days. And so they agreed that they would meet then.

Just one hour later, Stefi called Louise excitedly exclaiming, "I can't believe who I saw today agape. Dimitri is here! I cannot believe it . . . how can it be that he has not been here since you left some eight weeks ago and suddenly he turns up on the very first day you are here! I'm coming up now," Stefi laughed and seemed to appear with Yiannis at her gate in less time than it took for Louise to put the phone down on her!

They laughed and chatted, Louise explaining

what had happened that day, as they built a roaring log fire to keep out the evening's chill which had descended just that day.

As the days passed, Louise realised that she had never seen this place so deserted. The weather had turned, become quite wild and the whole area took on a deep sense of isolation and desolation as the winds grew stronger and stronger.

"Wild weather really is transformative," Louise explained to her friend as they sat with the children drinking hot tea in front of the fire to warm them after their cliff top walk.

She knew that the wild weather, coupled with the isolation was a reflection of where she needed to be ... alone, with herself, integrating the great rollercoaster of feelings and events she been experienced throughout the summer and autumn months. She knew that only to be immersed in this isolation, to be still and quiet, to listen to herself, to face things she had not yet been ready to face within her, was what would create the transformation within.

"Well, I'd better leave in case Dimitri does suddenly show up tonight," Stefi murmured, the deep love she felt for her friend so very evidently displayed across her features.

Louise knew already, that he would not. It was Tuesday and there had been no sign of him in the village. He had not called her and she had no intention of calling him. If they were supposed to meet again, then it would be.

"Stefi, I have seen what I needed to see," she said to her friend. "I have seen his love for me. There is no doubting it and now I must just trust that whatever is to come to pass for both our goods, will come to pass."

But even while she spoke these words, they both knew that she would love to spend just one more evening with him.

"I am sorry I wasn't here last night; I couldn't get back from the other job until today," Dimitri spoke gently as he stood before her now, surrounded by work colleagues at the hotel, shielded from the wild weather under a canopy.

Something had once again shifted within him and she knew instantly what it was. He had retreated to his head, the place of logic and reason, and the place to hide from the vulnerability of being within your heart. He looked so very tired, as if so many years had descended upon him in just a few days.

"I am just here today and then I must drive back again tomorrow evening," he continued. "I have college tonight in Iraklion and so won't be back here until around midnight. Should I call you when I'm on my way back and come and see you then?" he asked.

"Of course, if you are not too tired," she replied softly, turning to walk away. As she began to walk back down the slope toward her car she stopped and turned back toward him, sure she had heard him say something to her. Flickers of deep pain and turmoil within were etched across his face. Momentarily, his face broke into a grin and he went to step toward her, his hand outstretched . . . then something held him back.

As she lay alone in front of the fire that night, the boys exhausted and tucked up in bed, tears fell across her face once more.

She knew he would not call, would not come. The pain in his face had shown her that.

Hours later, as the dying embers of the fire faded, she walked outside onto her balcony and into the bitterly cold wind. She gazed up at the stars and called out to the Magus.

"Where are you?" she whispered against the dark of the night.

Taking a pen and paper she began to write:

> How in this moment may I see
> The beauty now beheld in thee;
> When I do dwell upon the cloud
> That sits amongst my heart so loud.
>
> The truth of you is flower's breath,
> Is song beheld, is life's full end;
> The deepest parts of laughter here
> Are mine and yours, the joy so near.
>
> I love you, know that this is true
> Forever am I held in you;
> And you in me my darling man
> As we now take each other's hand.
>
> Moment's scent I smell once more
> Your breath upon my cheek so sure;
> Your eyes bear deep into my soul
> As all our love once more unfolds.

*I want to run away from here
To be held so close, so very near,
By your arms so strong and sure,
And our love forever more.*

*You promised you would find me here,
You whispered to me loud and clear;
Never give up on me, I'll come
So you won't face the world alone.*

*And yet I stand here, so alone
I wait for you to take me home;
I choose right now to hold you sure,
Be held by you and loved once more.*

*I call you now 'cross time and space
To hold, fulfil your oath you made
To be beside me, love me once more,
And openly adore
Our sacred union . . . so sure.*

As she finished writing, Louise knew it was now time to face within her all that she had not been prepared to. Ahqulieah had arrived and it was now time to embrace the energy of this majestic, graceful, childlike and yet powerful woman.

So she prepared herself for what she knew would be the most significant and challenging seven days she had ever spent with anyone.

The days she was about to spend facing herself.

Every day that passed they walked together, her, her children, Stefi and Yiannis. They traversed the highest cliff tops, the wildest coastlines and encountered the roughest seas she had ever witnessed in Crete. By nightfall, once the children were tucked up in bed and she quite alone in front of the fire, the silence became her teacher.

Louise, who taught and advocated the healing powers of silence, finally took her own advice . . .

And it hurt . . .

And she wept . . .

And her heart screamed with the pain that tore her apart at the core of her being.

Hour after hour she watched the flames dancing in the dark of the night, desperately trying to understand the message that they must surely have for her.

Who was she?

How could she ever feel the extraordinary heights of that love she had felt with Adrian, and then Dimitri, again?

"For the only way that this is possible, is to open

your heart always to the greatest possibilities, the greatest experiences of the most exquisite bliss and the most extraordinary pain in the very same moment. The very thing that you ask others to do," she whispered to herself in the dying hours of the night.

She re-lived the very first moment she had experienced that exquisite bliss of love, those few moments that she and Adrian had had together on the streets of Dublin on that magical and mystical night two years earlier, before they had been pulled away from each other with no way of contacting one another again.

She remembered the pain on his face as he stood, motionless, on that dark and misty street, tears falling upon his face as she walked away from him.

They had both known deep within them that their journeys began there. Each one of their journeys was to take them on their own particular path.

Maybe one day she would understand exactly where his path had lead him. Maybe their paths would come full circle and back to each other, in the perfect moment.

"I will never forget you," he had whispered to her through their tears.

She recalled the months that followed as she had returned to England, utterly lost, bewildered, torn apart with the pain that was coursing through her.

She had believed that the pain she was experiencing then was because that love she had just touched with Adrian had been taken away from her, as he had been taken away from her.

It was as the months that followed began to pass that her incredible journey of miracles, synchronicities and synergies had unfolded about her.

This became her trail that she followed implicitly with the innocence and eyes of a child and with a heart so open.

She had no choice but to follow the call of her heart, her intuition which continued to surprise her with the twists and turns, the highs and lows of the amazing path that unfolded.

As the journey went on she met so many people around the globe who became so significant to her on this journey; as if characters playing out a role in her story.

She came to understand that the love she thought had been taken away from her had never left her.

For who can take away the love that is, in fact, yourself.

Adrian had been the most perfect and powerful mirror for her to feel the love within her. She was, quite literally, the love that she felt.

Every person she had met since then had taken her deeper and deeper into her heart, closer and closer to the truth of her story.

Without restraint she implored others to reside in their hearts, to open themselves to the exquisite experience of bliss and pain in the same moment, to the truth of the experience of life.

"For how can your amazing story truly unfold for you until you surrender to it, until you are brave enough to take that free fall dive into the unknown and embrace the miracles that unfold for you as you dwell in the most dangerous and yet the most exciting place you could ever possibly dwell in . . . the place of your heart? This is the true meaning of being alive, of the experience of life. All of the external pleasures that money can buy will never offer you the most exquisite gift of all . . . the gift of love."

As she stared into the fire, she realised that these words that she had spoken to so many people, were the very words she had so readily refused to face herself.

For it truly was a very challenging thought that the very person you had been searching for, for all of your life, and across all of the ages, was actually you!
"This is at once the most frightening and yet the most liberating place to be," she gasped as she watched the dying embers of the fire quite suddenly explode into a tirade of vibrant green flames.

She knew in that moment that the new life within the fire, that these green flames had just confirmed was the magic and the wisdom of the heart. She picked up a pen and wrote, in those magical moments, the poem that slipped so easily through her:

When time began the moment seemed a gift too rare to write,
For only in its constant stream could stories full and bright,
Be brought to all who sought to tread the many paths before,
And yet knew well, that time before, was time still left in store.

For how could we play game so grand, the notion of a life,
Until we felt within our hearts that there could be such strife;
And what a lark, a mischief true, to tell yourself so well,
That life's full end is on you now, when truth will yet unfurl.

And what a truth this is indeed, the grandest story yet,
Of miracles within your hand as you do see them set;
For you indeed are all things now, the ground below your feet;
The lightning bolt that streaks the sky, the strength where rivers meet.

The torrent of the hurricane as its power unleashes all,
The sun so strong across your cheek as dusk begins to fall.
The time for life is ever here, its magic in you now;
For you, my dear, are magic true as life does show you how.

*So breathe so deep and laugh so loud for all you know right here,*
*Is all you ever sought to seek when you called life so dear.*
*Upon the outset of the game you deftly drew aloft,*
*Until the moment you would wake and time, my dear, would stop.*

*And in that waking gift so great would shake you to the core,*
*As love of ages, full and bright, returns to you once more.*

She sighed deeply, feeling the message of this poem course through her.

The following day, with this understanding rooted within her entire being, the knowing that the love of the ages that she had sought to find for so long was, in fact, herself, she left Crete . . .

And she left Dimitri, the man she loved beyond measure, and to whom she was eternally grateful for bringing her to a place of such understanding.

# England

## November 2008

"So, I wonder what today will bring." Cherry smiled at Louise as they sat together talking about all that had happened while she was in Crete.

"The most amazing thing of all," Louise said, "is the meaning of the hedgehog that I saw at the beginning of the trip. It is good that I hadn't known what it meant whilst I was there. It was great confirmation for me of how I decided to face all that I had to face by being so still with me."

Cherry was intrigued. "Go on," she said expectantly.

"The hedgehog teaches defence against negativity. It shows you how to love life and walk with a sense of lightness and wonder. It shows you how to act with tenacity and strength to get things done, to face and balance emotions. It is there to ensure that you take time out for you and to show you how to be confident and move with strength."

"Pretty spot on then," Cherry laughed while Louise hopped up onto the bed and closed her eyes, relaxing and preparing for what was to come.

"I should just mention," Louise quickly added, "that I have had an intense pain in my right arm since I woke this morning. It is extremely difficult to find a position to be comfortable with it."

"Oh I think we are about to find out what that is all about," Cherry added mischievously.

"Where are you," Louise heard Cherry's distant voice.

She was frozen with horror. She was standing at the top of an open chasm, hot sand between her toes, desert all about her and a thick black acrid smoke rising from the square shaped chasm before her. She could barely make out the shape of the large stone slabs which descended in perfect symmetry before her, deep into what seemed an abyss.

The Magus was standing with her, gripping her hand tightly, his piercing blue eyes striking a chord to her heart as the hot desert wind whipped his long unruly hair about his face.

"We must go down. You must let me take you back in there," he said, gently urging her forward into the chasm.

"Where are you Louise?" she heard Cherry's ever more distant voice, "tell me."

"He wants me to go down there with him," she barely whispered. "I can't see anything but the dark mist that is emanating from the pit in front of us. The smell is so awful. It's the smell of acrid burning flesh."

But it was the noise that was striking the core of her, making her recoil with terror. For all she could hear was the clicking of thousands of beetles, rising from somewhere deep beneath her, from within the black mist that he was leading her down into.

"It's okay, I am with you and nothing will happen to you, trust me," he said as he took a simple rope of silken cord and fastened it around their two wrists so that they could not be parted in the dark.

As they stepped down through the black mist and into an enormous crystal chamber, the noise grew to a pitch which almost deafened them.

Her jaw fell open as, standing before them now, was a stunning sarcophagus. They were clearly in the centre of a burial chamber and the sarcophagus depicted a beautiful girl, an Egyptian goddess.

Something was tugging her, pulling her toward the sarcophagus and she found herself walking into it, in a trance like state, a great terror infusing her.

"What's happening now?" Cherry asked from a distance.

Silent screams were coursing through her body, the body of the girl within the sarcophagus she realised. For it was as if they had become one. She was now, quite literally this girl, with all of her dying thoughts flooding Louise's consciousness.

"They thought I was dead but I'm alive. They have buried me alive!" Her voice was barely audible.

So many crystals surrounded her within that tomb. She had plenty of room to move her limbs and as she did so, she felt excruciating pain within her right arm. It had been strapped with great black iron strapping to weigh it down. It felt as if it no longer belonged to her, as if some evil was lurking within it, until she understood that something within her arm was the target of the scarab beetles she now heard entering the sarcophagus.

She was filled with horror. A tall man stood to the left of the sarcophagus, a broad cold smile upon his face. Here was the perpetrator of this burial she knew in that instant.

This man was not interested in whether she was alive or dead. What he wanted was to capture the codes of light which were darting about within her right arm now, codes which carried secrets of creation. He believed that the beetles could digest them and bring them back to him. He was mistaken.

In her state of terror, she suddenly became quite numb, quite determined. She withdrew her arm from the black strapping. Her body was now entirely made up of white light. She could hear a man crying out above her sarcophagus, a man who had just discovered what was happening, a man who loved her deeply, who looked so like the Magus.

Oblivious now to the beetles crawling all over her body and the screams her earthly body was emitting, she began to incise codes upon the underside of the sarcophagus, codes in an ancient language, as she felt the Magus next to her, whispering to her.

"This is about the length that people will go to find the codes" he spoke quietly. "Endeth am ith min. When you were entombed, as your lover, your partner, I dug a pit next to you. I buried myself and called the beetles to me away from you. As they ate into me, I screamed my love for you. For forty days I suffered while you incised the codes within the sarcophagus, ancient codes of light. I walked out of my body and into the sarcophagus to be with you. Together we merged as one light being. We walked out of the sarcophagus, through a portal, and found ourselves back in the little forest, in our little hut. We knew that we had passed the test of our love. This never happened. It is but another story we created in order to bring about another level of alchemy. We brought back yet another code with us. Find the strength to complete it now beautiful girl," he implored her.

As she wrote at speed, committing these codes to the underside of the sarcophagus, she felt the codes of creation come through as vibrant and alive, moving particles, molecular structures of light.

As she finished writing, in what had seemed an eternity, he whispered to her, "Now we can leave." Still bound at the wrists, they stood up as beings of light, and walked out of the sarcophagus to see that that black smoke had lifted and the chamber was now turning back to a brilliant golden light.
 Amazing and intricate drawings were appearing on the walls in front of them.
 "Who are you?" Cherry asked from a distance. "Who is this Egyptian goddess?"
 She turned to look at the Magus who asked her to kneel at the side of the sarcophagus.
 "Honour her," he said. "She is you. Tell her what happened to her and why and what has now occurred. She is Nefertiti."

The shock registered within her now; shock and yet deep knowing. How could it be that she could remember this girl's dying days and yet nothing that preceded them, nothing except for the bond she felt for the man who was her lover?

A shaft of brilliant light appeared now within the golden chamber and began to speak to them both as it took on different, continually changing forms and shapes.

"A shapeshifter," she thought to herself, although she knew that this was far more than a shapeshifter. The electromagnetic charge within the chamber was nothing she had ever experienced.

"Where is this place?" she whispered to the Magus.

"Very, very deep," he replied as he began to give her the precise name and location of where they were.

The light took on a spectacular form and, instantly she knew they were standing before the centre of the universal source.

As it offered them a scroll it began to speak.

"Open the scroll and discover the most amazing story of all time. This is a place and time unknown to man because man is unknown to it," it began.

"Forged in a chasm of fire of all that is, I am the most extraordinary being. I am all that is. I am the light that you could not possibly conceive, imagine. It is my pleasure to play all of these games. The story I have, no one could ever imagine. It would seem ridiculous. It is through the radiation, the intense molecular being, that there is a dimensional structure which is a mirror. This mirror is fractal and replays back to everyone, all that they have been, all that they are, and all that they ever could be. It is like a kaleidoscope. I am at the centre of the kaleidoscope. I am a hologram, a prism, I am at the centre of a hexagram. This prism has grown ever bigger, ever lighter, ever brighter. Look back at the story that was written. Look at me, what do you see?"

The pain in her arm became so intense at this point. Tears of pain worked their way across her face as the figure in front of them changed shape yet again. The deep blood red writing on the scroll kept appearing and then disappearing before them as they watched intently.

The light quite suddenly and dramatically expanded within the chamber. All that she could now see was the figure before them and the dark features of the man by her side.

She glanced down at the silken cord still tightly bound around their wrists, to see codes of light dancing, alive within her right arm.

"Codes of creation," the source before them cried out as it laughed.

"The writing on the scroll?" Louise whispered.

"Only the truth can mark the scroll. Some have tried to burn it but this is not possible. Many have tried to use it for their own purpose, their own end. The scroll carries all of creation. Only one can wield the power of the scroll and only those in light and grace can access the scroll. It can never be destroyed. It hides all and only reveals that which the reader is allowed to see. Ancient Egyptians knew of the scroll and searched for the codes contained within it. There was much ritual and ceremony around it," the source continued.

"Who . . . who can wield the power of the scroll?" she asked.

"The Undeth Meron."

"Who are the Undeth Meron?" she implored, staggered at what she was hearing now.

"They are the origins of all that is. They are a high council, a race of beings of colossal power and magnitude. They are androgynous beings who created the one who can wield the power of the scroll, the same one who commands the Undeth Meron. He, who is their champion, is the greatest human form in which 'the one that is' has ever been embodied."

Without another word, the source before them disappeared as quickly as it had appeared.

"Come with me Louli," the Magus urged her gently as they began to climb the cold stone steps toward the sunlight high above them. As they reached the desert once more, a great stone slab shut tight across the chamber.

She caught sight of an emblem engraved into the stone slab, an emblem of a very distinctive shape and design with codes of light moving about within it, and then the sand blew across it and all evidence of where they had just been was gone.

The Magus cut the silken cord from around their wrists and they stepped forward and through a void of moving energy particles which had appeared before them in the desert, a kind of stargate.

Instantly, she could smell the fires, hear the

druids laughing, the birds chatter and feel the gentle breeze upon her cheek. The little leather skinned hut stood on the edge of the forest and her Magus by her side.

As she looked up into his eyes an inexplicable bond wound about them both, as if the very journey they had just been on had created a new sense of union, of alchemy. It seemed as if their very essence as it came together created a third energy, a third being.

"We are home," he smiled at her.

"Yes, we are," she replied, a great peace enveloping her.

And then Louise began, under Cherry's questioning, to unearth some quite astounding information.

"Wrap this around you." Cherry wrapped a blanket around Louise's shoulders as, shaking she climbed off the bed. As she began to drink a very hot, sweet tea that Cherry had made for her, they exchanged shocked expressions.

"Cherry," Louise whispered.

"I know what you are about to say," Cherry replied. "Some of this can be written now into your current book, but there is much which is certainly for the third book. The links are extraordinary!"

"Yes they are," she said, still shaking. "The great awakeners who had all been a part of Egyptian ritual, priesthood and ceremony, who are all within the Celtic legends of the ages, the Rosicrucian origins, the heretic pharaoh, the clarion calls, the codes of light, the script, and the one who wields the power of the Undeth Meron. And that is just the beginning . . ."

"Louise, who is this man I can see here in the tea? He has appeared with a castle, lightly bearded, long unruly dark hair, quite like the figure of Jesus. Then he appears in a hotel, working with his hands."

Lee had been Louise's good friend for some years now. They had found each other just after Louise had returned from meeting Adrian.

Totally aware of his clairvoyant abilities since the age of twelve, he had been reading tarot cards, tea leaves and the crystal ball for all of his adult life, and only recently charging people for doing so.

His accuracy with events, names, dates and his ability to really determine outcomes was quite extraordinary, so much so that many of Louise's friends had become his customers. Louise knew that everybody had this skill as it was a natural state for everyone.

However, she also knew that for the people of the world to accept this, they would first have to embrace the fact that they were born to create miracles. This was their birthright; to be alchemists.

"And this goes directly against the grain of everything that we have been brought up to believe. All it takes is to understand the process of transforming your energy into a lighter state of being, of playing the game of life instead of being its victim," she mused.

Not only had Lee embraced his great abilities from an early age, he had also researched and experimented and become very open to growing in the area he was destined to explore . . . alchemy. And here was their great common passion!

"He is someone you have just spent some time with. He cannot get you out of his head. You have really challenged him. There is an inexplicable attraction and power to your union; a very strong mental and physical attraction. It's as if the hand of fate holds a globe of light, a lantern between you both. This meeting was meant to occur between you Louise. Who is he?"

"Ah, this would be Dimitri" Louise sighed, smiling, not at all surprised that Lee had picked up on him straight away. "I met him in Crete this summer; we spent almost four weeks together. It was a challenging four weeks for us both. Instant love. He looked so like Adrian."

"I see him in a windswept country. Devastation is happening all around him and he is thinking about you. He is not ready for a relationship with you yet Louise. He is ambitious, working hard and saving money so that he can travel the world. He has a passion to see the world, because he is searching for something. He knows that the relationship you have had is sacred and special, but he is not ready to acknowledge this or even recognise it at times. Why do I feel that there is no contact between you now?"

Louise explained why.

"It will re-establish itself," Lee continued. "Most importantly, I see a soul union, a man who appears to you through the mist, completely out of the blue when you least expect it. This union is completion, as if you two have been together in all lifetimes, across the ages and you come back here together in the perfect moment. Opposite forces creating union.

He is scarred; he bears the mark of Excalibur from another lifetime. He is a warrior, an immensely powerful man and has come here for a very specific reason. He has prayed for you as much as you have prayed for him.

This man, Louise, appears to you through your mist when you are both ready. The mist that I see in the crystal ball is your self-awareness, and your ability to remove all preconceptions about him.

He will only appear when you are ready to embrace and value the relationship that you will have. The mist is fading now and the gap between you is closing. There is also something critical for you to understand before he can come to you. When you two come together, it's as if your very essence, the joining of each of you, will create a third energy, a new energy, an alchemical energy.

I see you as two giant keys and you unlock deep held knowledge within each other. Only he has the key to the knowledge in you and only you in him. This man comes to you in your dreams Louise. You meet him in your dreams before you do in this reality. The initial 'A' is here for him again."

They laughed. It was always the initial 'A' that appeared. She, once again, sensed a deep symbolic meaning.

Louise thought of the Magus. She didn't feel ready to discuss this with anyone right now.

"Louise, Queen Nefertiti's head is in your tea. This is the second time this has happened. Do you remember this happened about eight months ago?"

Louise was stunned, she had completely forgotten.

"She is an amazing omen. She means feminine power, great manipulation of that power for the good of all, strength and a great ruler. The initial 'A' is connected to her too."

"Lee, do you know who Nefertiti was married to?" she asked quietly.

When Lee replied that he did not she went on, "Amenhotep the Fourth, more commonly known as Akhenaten. He was the pharaoh who was declared heretic for creating a new city, Tel El-Amarna, which he cited between the extreme religious warring factions within Egypt of that time. Akhenaten was the first Pharaoh of Egypt. He and Nefertiti had been brought up together, been prepared from childhood to become husband and wife and create a whole new possibility of life within Egypt. They were distinctly different in shape, stature and height from anyone in the Egyptian world at that time. He was only eighteen years old when he became king and ruled for seventeen and a half years until he and Nefertiti died. He set out to eradicate all the different occults and put in place a religion where one simple God was understood. He used the image of the sun to do so, to act as a representation of God as a stepping stone to bring people closer to the truth of what the energy of God really was. That's why his whole city, Tel El-Amarna, was oriented toward the sun, and Sirius.

'In this new religion we will have no more lies,

only truthfulness,' he has been recorded as saying, 'You don't need priests. God is within you. There is only one God and you can access that God within yourself.'

Akhenaten became very unpopular with the priests, because he removed all of their power. As he was a pacifist he also enraged the military, said to be the most powerful global army at that time and who wanted to conquer the world. The people of Egypt turned against him as they did not like his intention for them to honour only one God.

The circumstances of the deaths of Akhenaten and Nefertiti have never really been proven. According to the Egyptian records, Akhenaten was poisoned by both the military and priesthood combined and then buried in a sarcophagus. The city of Tel El-Amarna was then removed stone by stone to extinguish any evidence of this man.

Other documents suggest something quite different. They recount his true origins and his ability to remain in the sarcophagus alive for some 2000 years. As for Nefertiti, no one knows what happened to her. There are certain 'facts' recorded which are completely contradictory."

"How do you know all this Louise?" Lee asked.

Louise began to tell Lee of the regression experience she had undergone with Cherry some weeks before, of the research she had carried out since and of her shock as she had begun to unearth information which matched with some of the facts she was being told during the regression.

"I didn't even know who Nefertiti was really," she continued. "The thing is Lee, Akhenaten created a mystery school. I read about it in Drunvalo Melchizedek's book 'The Ancient Secret of The Flower of Life'. Within this school he took some 300 people through a process (very aligned to The Alchemies of Horus taught by Isis, who was an ancient Egyptian Goddess) to a state of immortality. When he died, it is said that these people, the Tat Brotherhood, travelled to Masada in Israel and formed a group called The Essene Brotherhood. They believed that the next step back to humanity understanding its true immortal origins, was to facilitate the birth of a human who would grow through the process taught within the mystery school and go on to demonstrate that it is possible to be killed and not die. This person they chose, we know by the name of Jesus of Nazareth. His mother Mary and father Joseph were part of the inner circle of the Essene Brotherhood. They used the alchemies of Horus to create a sacred sexual union to conceive Jesus. By doing so, Mary would be able to carry and give birth to a baby of much higher vibrational energy than the average human at that time. It was this energy at birth that provided the foundation of his path to immortality."

Lee was listening very intently now.

"Do you think that the 'A' that has appeared next to Nefertiti could be Akhenaten. Could this then be linked to my 'A'?" she asked.

"I don't know. We will see," he spoke quietly, knowing who else they suspected her 'A' to be.

# England

## Christmas Eve 2008

"Let's stop peeling vegetables and head for the pub now," Louise laughed with Charlie as her friend readily agreed, throwing the dishes into the sink.

How Louise always loved Christmas Eve and as her boys were with their father this year, she had time to relax and prepare for the following day . . . a day that would see twenty of her family with her!

As they sat chatting with friends in the pub, they bathed in the energy of merriment. Everyone was so full of the Christmas spirit . . . literally, she and Charlie joked together!

Her thoughts drifted momentarily to Dimitri and she wondered how he was and what he would be doing for Christmas. She had nothing but love in her heart for this man and knew that her only desire was that he was happy, wherever he was.

How wonderful it would be, if the universe conspired to bring them together again, to become friends, to talk and to bathe in that amazing connection that drew them inexplicably to each other.

Even as she pondered this, she knew that it didn't actually matter whether she saw him again. For the only thing that really mattered was that she loved him, just as he was, for all he had brought to her across time and space, for however much he was aware that he had brought her . . . or not!

For it was most certainly Dimitri who had shown her the true meaning of surrender; of unconditional love. She knew that he was always with her and she yearned in that moment, with all her soul, that he would find his true purpose, his true light and his true love . . .

For he deserved it.

Later that evening as she sat in bed writing her book, writing about him, her heart suddenly nudged her in that all too familiar fashion, to call him.

Without hesitation she picked up the phone, remembering that they hadn't spoken since she had last left him in Crete.

"Ella agape," she heard him say, almost sing, in his deep dulcet tones. His heart leapt as he heard her voice. How long it had seemed since they had last spoken and, as ever, she made him feel light, her energy drawing forth the child within him.

They laughed together and talked at length for what seemed hours but was, in fact, only forty minutes. She spoke of their book being nearly finished, of its content and intent. Her heart was filled with her love for him as she felt him blush at the thought of so many hearing her declaration of his beauty.

He really had been the most incredible reflection for her to embrace her sacred union with herself. She knew that every time he had seemed to walk away from her it had really been her walking away from the love of herself. All he had done was be the mirror for her to see that.

But now, here he was telling her of his planned visit to Holland in May and how he would love to come and see her too.

"Maybe we could visit your castle in Edinburgh," she had teased him, remembering deep within her soul the reason why she so yearned to take him there.

As he readily agreed, she wondered what magic the universe had in store for them.

How she would love to share with him the many links of Edinburgh to the mysteries of King Arthur, of Magdalene and Christ, and of the great Celtic battles of mythology.

How she would love to stand in the uppermost turret with him, where so much had come to pass for them both and have the opportunity to witness any recollection within him.

There was a deep sense of peace that passed between them in those moments and, above all, an absolute bond that surpassed all attempt to articulate.

For, how is it possible to articulate a love that runs so deep within you, about you, that the very mention of it brings you to a place of great pain, such bliss and yet an overriding peace in the same instant.

"This is the very place where so many fear to tread and yet, without treading its path, the purpose of life is lost. This is the sacred truth," she whispered to herself, tears coursing down her face in joy as she felt that love wash through her entire being.

She felt so blessed to have touched it once more. She felt so honoured that Dimitri, as Adrian before him, had stepped forward to play such a significant role in her journey to discover the sacred truth, the sacred union of the love of the self.

And, as she reflected on his final words to her, his promise to call her soon and desire to stay with her in May, she realised that he had already brought her the greatest gift that was possible to ever bring another. The gift of unconditional love. The love of self.

And she thought of the Magus, and she wrote:

> If life were a moment for eyes that can see,
> What would the moment bring only to thee?
> The knowing that magic is just where you tread,
> And all of life's mysteries are thoughts you had set.
>
> In game so glorious, stories foretold,
> Of chivalrous notions, of laughter and gold;
> Of deeds so pure and noble in stead,
> And alchemy's hand as your heart weaves its thread.
>
> Now as you close your eyes, listen so sure,
> The door of your heart will impart even more.
> It calls to you endlessly, whispers your name,
> And tells you your journey, your place in your game.
>
> Listen so carefully, never be swayed,
> For only in hearing can miracles be made.
> For now as you enter the realm of your dreams,
> All of this magic is here at your means.

# England

## New Year's Eve

"What a great way to spend New Year's Eve," Louise and Lee agreed.

She had been invited to so many parties, dinners, drinks and events in London. What she truly wanted to do was to be very quiet, with herself, and celebrate what was to come within her.

She had called Lee just a few days before and he had felt the same.

"There really is something very magical about having a reading with you tonight," she continued, "in fact it's always magical having a reading with you Lee".

They laughed together and chatted about many things.

"Shall we begin?" he asked. "Louise . . ."

She knew that this great silent pause of his meant something significant, it always did.

"I have never seen this before . . . there is a city rising up out of the ocean. This is a city that was long forgotten. It is as if you are rediscovering it, reclaiming it. The work you are about to do around this is new and groundbreaking."

He was silent again.

"I see you in a manor house, with castle ruins. I see your partner coming to you in time. He is a warrior, solid in strength and ready for you. He is marked by King Arthur's sword Excalibur. A dragon stands by his side, which represents his power, his wisdom and his courage. Your union transcends time. It is a very unusual union and one of grace and courage. The ceremony to bind it is like a medieval re-enactment. That's how I see it. Now, you know I don't like using this language," Lee laughed, "but I have to say what I am being told. He is your knight and only he can claim you."

They both laughed.

"Now, the fact that he is a knight is of great importance. Ancient script and codes are appearing now, codes which push the boundaries of any comprehension. There is an energy surfacing. Louise . . ."

She waited, anticipating what was coming.

"It's an energy around your third book which has just exploded in front of me in a ball of fire. It is very important to protect your ideas around this book. Listen carefully to what I am saying," he stressed.

"This book is going to uncover something. Even you don't know yet what that is. You know parts of it, but there is a lot more to come. It is necessary that you have had to go through certain learnings so you are truly ready to protect the information that is coming. You are the key and you must protect what will be released to you now," he continued.

"It is at this time that a huge shift of energy will occur around you, around your partner who is coming. You and he together will unlock information, codes. This book is on the edge of creation. It is a doorway between opposite poles of mankind, polarities of fear. All of the elements are present within it. It is encoded with moving creation. It is quite literally alchemy and magic. You must protect your ideas around it Louise," he emphasised once more.

"Wow, what a way to start a New Year! No pressure then." Louise laughed as they finished the reading.

Lee, however, was not laughing. "Louise, this is serious. I have never seen this before. I know you. I know how open and trusting you are. I know how you stand in your truth and share so much. But there is a time when that is not appropriate and this is it. Do not share anything with anyone. Please listen to me!"

As she put down the phone and headed for Cherry's, who had agreed to give her a healing that evening, Lee's words struck deep within her heart. He was right, of course. She shared so much always, believing that this was not her information, but that of everyone.

She also considered in that moment that the impact of information, stories within a book for example, if given ahead of time, was greatly reduced.

And so, she determined that night, to only share the information arising with the two people who had been uncovering so much with her, two people that she absolutely knew would not use any of that information in any way outside of her writing.

Later that night, as she committed that dedication to fire, together with her determination to bring this third book into being, she watched the flames in her fireplace turn very green indeed!

# Tintagel Castle, Cornwall

## 2nd February 2009

"Tintagel, meaning fortress of the narrow entrance," Louise read in her guide book as she scaled the heights of the medieval castle perched on top of a sheer cliff rising from the boulder strewn sea shore far below.

The bitterly cold wind whipped about her, her hair lashing against her face in the icy ocean spray which seemed to somehow scale the heights from far below.

The sun was high in the sky, caressing her senses as if to provide the perfect backdrop, the perfect reminder of the deep polarity of the essence of life.

She smiled as she pondered on the fact that the rest of Britain was completely snowed in and yet, somehow, she had managed to reach here the night before leaving the snow trailing in her wake.

"Lucky I followed my intuition and left Sunday night, not this morning," she thought to herself as she steadied herself in the ever increasing torrent of wind.

She had been so determined to get here, to be able to bathe in the Arthurian energy of Tintagel, legendary birthplace of King Arthur, to finish writing her second book. This book was one she had never expected to write. This was the love story of her and Dimitri, of her and the Magus.

Most importantly, this was the love story of her with herself, her sacred union. For she now truly understood that to trust yourself, to know yourself to be worthy of the greatness of life and love is to know that you are never abandoned, never alone but, rather, extraordinarily held in the greatest love of all time.

The love of all the ages.

The love of the one, the love of you.

How fitting, she smiled to herself, that the energy of Tintagel, mythologies birthplace of the earthly King Arthur, was to be where she would conclude this book. For it was the mythological tales of this great king that held such clues adeptly coded deep within the search for the Holy Grail that revealed the truth of the real search ... for the meaning of life.

The same truth cleverly hidden in so many codes and scripts across so many stories of old, stories she now firmly believed to be those of the game of life, the trail.

All of the ancient cultures, secret societies, timeless scripts held these so called secrets.

So many great teachers, fictitious or otherwise, across time and space had explicitly laid these codes bare for all to see; those such as Aristotle, Shakespeare, Ahkenaten, Jesus, Einstein, Socrates, Arthur, Da Vinci, Michelangelo, Gibran and William Wallace.

Their words had been distorted, hidden and misrepresented in perfection so that the truth they spoke remained hidden until the world was ready to see it; to embrace its simplicity.

For, the sacred state of unconditional love, of grace, was both simplicity and alchemy in its greatest form.

"This was the true meaning of life, to finally remember that we never were separated from the great love that is our self," she whispered against the torrent of wind unleashed upon her now.

"What a crazy and miraculous game life is. What fun to delude ourselves that we are separated from love, only to spend our entire life searching for the truth that we are that love, the truth that we knew from the outset," she pondered.

As she reached the gale-lashed summit of the island, she looked back down below her to the tiny bridge at the foot of the incredibly steep and craggy staircase that still remained, connecting the island to the mainland and the two halves of King Arthur's court.

Her vision strayed back along the mainland to the hotel manor house where she was staying. It stood majestic and alone against the bleak landscape.

She felt instant warmth sweep through her as she recalled the enormous burning log fires in its great chivalric hall.

Fleetingly, as she turned back to the steep cliff's edge overhanging the ocean, she thought of the connection of Tintagel to Arthur's seat in Edinburgh, of Edinburgh Castle and she thought of Dimitri.

Then, quite instantly, as her thoughts drifted to the journey that the Magus was leading her on, the man she knew and loved so well, she seemed to lose her footing.

Her vision swayed. She turned away from the cliff edge, her back facing the ocean, to see a landscape devoid of any buildings, any people, any castles.
She knew that, although this coastline seemed identical to the Tintagel one she had just been standing on, she had just stepped into another lifetime, another reality.

The sky was so dark, so very stormy and the rain and wind lashed upon her face as she drew her long velvet hooded robe close about her.

Where was she? What was this time and space? She gazed toward the angry sky as she felt excitement and misery simultaneously tearing at the core of her.

As she looked upon a brilliant shaft of light carving the only break in the darkened skies, she knew this was where she had just arrived from, and in that moment she yearned to be home.

She could feel the incredible power of alchemy within her. She knew she had the ability to create many forms of alchemy and yet she had no idea how to use it.

She looked around her, down to the jagged coast line below, the craggy descents and the caves filling with the wild ocean waves roaring against the sound of the storm around her.

People began to appear in the distance now. People dressed as she was, in long simple hooded robes, pulling the robes around them to shield them from the torrential weather as they walked toward her.

She gazed back toward the mainland in wonder as the most incredible scene appeared miraculously before her, as if completely out of nowhere. A trail of stunning silver pebbles was forming a path from her feet to across the horizon, illuminating a way forward through the stormy mist. As she followed the path, she could hear the others calling her by her name, "Ethbeneren".

She could clearly distinguish their voices against the wind as they, too, walked toward the path.

A great city of onyx stone was beginning to form now, materialising at the climax of the path. This city felt to her as if it held every memory and record across the ages of all the great deeds, the magnificent times and the host of possibilities that ever had been and ever could be.

Thousands of eagles were circling over its vast, spectacular walls as it loomed before her, growing in splendour with every step she took toward it.

As she and the others approached the drawbridge which had appeared before the city's great wooden gates, she saw a tall, slim man walking across the bridge toward her, his long dark unruly hair billowing behind him in the wild winds, an eagle flying closely by his shoulder. Her heart leapt, it sang, for she knew this man so well.

"In cath elath im anor. You know me," the Magus called out to her, his striking blue eyes laughing as he took her hand tightly and led her and the others over the bridge.

The great iron hinged gates swung open and a brilliant white light, so extraordinarily bright, dazzled them as they stepped over the threshold into the city.

She knew this place, the magic of Camelot so deeply rooted in its energy, and as she heard the familiar sound of the deep and husky alchemical voice booming from within its walls, she knew she had come home.

Louise's heart was infused with the absolute miracle of life as she gazed out towards the ocean. How alive and vibrant the wind made her feel as it seemed to whisper her beauty to the universe.

The sun caressed her cheek and the snow began to fall, gently at first, tiny promises of miracles adorning her hair.

She threw back her head and laughed, her voice calling the great Arthurian energy to envelop her in its mystery and magic.

She looked to the heavens and smiled. How was it possible that people could not see their beauty in the magnificence set out about her now?

As the snow fell harder, the sense of alchemy grew within her.

She was so excited, so passionately in love.

"For, what is love?" she called out to the ocean below her as she began to walk back toward the warmth of the hotel fires.

"Love is you," the ocean roared behind her, embracing her with its laughter.

"And you," she called, blowing a kiss to her lover. "For what greater lover could I find than the love of the ocean, of the skies, of the wind, of the stars, of the fire and of the earth beneath my feet?" she sang.

"Help me bring the world back to knowing their lover," she beseeched as a flash of light streaked across the darkening skies.

Smiling, she headed for cover.

"It really has been amazing to complete my book here," she laughed with a friend on the phone at 2 am.

The only friend who she could speak to at that time in the morning was in Australia and they talked about the polarity of the weather they were experiencing in that moment.

"And has anything exciting occurred?" her friend asked her now.

"Yes," she whispered, "but I am confused."

"Why?" her friend replied.

"Because I am beginning to understand how I must create the space for the heart to use the head, and yet it is only the magical energy of the heart, the alchemy of love that can bring immortality. Uncovering the alchemy of love as you know, is my purpose."

She lay in her bed. She could not sleep.

Why did she feel so confused? Because she was in love and yet, in that state of love, she had been challenged, challenged by a man she had not expected to meet here as she finished writing. He was so like her. She was shocked at their synergies. She felt an extraordinary magnetic pull towards him, and yet, something had left her deeply confused.

She felt a third energy, the energy of alchemy, that had been born in their meeting and she had no idea where this would lead.

The way he spoke with her, sang to her, challenged her, admired her, laughed with her, honoured her and teased her, had moved her to the very core.

It was not new to her.
He was not new to her.

As she had watched him play his guitar and sing to her that evening, the words of the song he dedicated to her, questioning her very soul, she felt such love in her heart.

She had wanted to reach out and touch him, to tell him that he was so safe now with her, that he could free fall dive into the vulnerability of his heart and explore the immortality of all things with her in that place.

And yet she hadn't.

Great honour passed between them and great space had been created.

She crept out of bed and strode to the window, gazing out across the moonlit ocean. Her hand reached out for a pen and paper and she began to write a poem to him that slipped so effortlessly through her now . . .

For only in the moments when darkness dawns through light,
And chasms forge within the mind as knowing sees full sight,
Does truth be nobly honoured here amongst the heady clouds,
And we do see the beauty of our many hours.

A teacher is a master that I behold in you;
That master is a child once more as all to him is new.
With eyes alive with laughter and mystery in his stead,
As he doth lead a merry dance with every step he treads.

And yet that mystery so sure is offered here to you,
For in his heart, if truth be said, he offers ages through.
His energy so bright and clear is all I sought to find,
When I once looked deep in my heart and asked what could be mine.

And so I'll love him evermore this man who knows me well,
And wonder always what's in store as miracles unfurl.
For evidence of what we seek alludes us oh so sure,
Until the day, when in our heart, we see with eyes once more.

**T**ears fell upon her face as she drove home in the snow. Every road she tried to take was closed and deserted. It was as if the universe was directing her back to where she had set out from. Back to the ocean, back to the magical Arthurian energy, back to him.

She kept driving until, many hours later, she reached her home ... and for the first time she knew that this was not home.

She gazed at the two tiny figures standing on a heath land looking out across the ocean as the moon carved a path of light across its crest. The cosmos seemed to dance above them as a shooting star brought them the promise of their every wish.

How this painting of his had captured the very essence of him, she mused.

What was its message to her?
To trust him, to trust life and to create the space for him to come to her.
To wish for him to come to her.
To remember what he had shown her.
To only grant her wishes, space to exist.

Surely if she could do this now, she had embraced the power of the wisdom of the head.

Surely if he could trust her, trust his heart and create the space for her to love him from her heart, then he had embraced the wisdom of the heart.

How? The answer was so clear. He could see the magical message through her writing, just as she could see the magical message in his painting.

"Beauty is in the eye of the beholder," he had said . . . and he was right.

And so, with her wish clearly defined within her heart, she sent him her message.

As she scaled the heights of the North Surrey Downs, the wind whispering to her as the sun shrouded her in its early morning light, her heart was torn apart.

On and on she walked, so totally alone ... and yet all of the elements held her, felt her deep turmoil as she wrestled with the notion of what was occurring within her now.

Oh, she knew so well that it was only the state of unconditional love in its greatest form that could bring about the metaphysical change she was experiencing in this moment. For she felt as if her entire being was on the verge of spontaneous combustion.

The energy that lifted her now, surrounded her and whispered so gently to her, served to root her even further within her heart.

As she stood so high upon the cliff edge she began to rock, the tears tearing her apart at the core of her being.

She gazed up toward the sky and began to sing the words of the message the Magus had sent her some eighteen months before.

A deep understanding flooded her consciousness as she recognised the Magus' message in the words spoken to her by the man who had challenged her so deeply in Cornwall, the man she had come to love.

"The sound of love is a frequency, love to my musical ear," the Magus had told her. This man had been so very particular in emphasising that this frequency of the sound of love was 'her' frequency.

And yet, her frequency must be his, for they were the same one, the same being, two parts of the same whole.

The pain of that separation coursed through her once more as she fell to her knees on the edge of the deep ravine below.

She called out to the wind, to the starry heavens, to the sun and to all that ever had been the union of these two to hold her now and unite her with the extraordinary man who was her.

For in this dimension, this realm, he carried the energy of Arthur once more.

The day passed with her barely able to see. Her vision blurred, her body burnt with a fever and yet she, so very cold, took to her bed.

Her heart implored her to write, knowing that the time was now, for the next part of this incredible journey to be committed to paper and to be made manifest.

She had no idea what would flow through her as she began to write.

She read the letter containing the message she had sent to him once more, its beauty striking a chord to the heart of her.

How honouring she was of this man and how she loved him so. For how could she not? He was she, and she was he.

She watched the little video of him and she wept. His voice, as he sang in the video, touched something so deep within her remembrance, a recall of a distant age past. An age where nobility, honour and love were so eloquently entwined to provide a great stage for the sacred union.

What would become of these two now?

# The Wish

The phone rang.

Three simple words were uttered.

As she listened to those words, time stood still. All that she ever had been and ever would be was forged within those three small words.

"It's me again."

The voice was that of her lover across time and space.

"I love you. Thank you for having the courage to be in this moment with me. Thank you, my dear, for trusting me with your heart as I now trust you with mine. Let's do what we came here to do together. Let's create this third energy, born of our sacred union . . . right now."

**A**s she reached up to hold his face in her hands, the power and majesty of the waves crashing about them, the tears flowing across their faces were tiny droplets of miracles reflecting their love for each other.

Their energy left their bodies and met at a great height. An extraordinary birth of alchemy illuminated the entire moonlit sky, the ocean and the mountain side.

Love was born in its greatest form and these two pledged once more their oath to each other; the oath they had taken at the beginning of time.

Standing in the centre of the labyrinth, rose petals fell about them as they put the rings from Edinburgh upon their fingers and publicly declared their oath to each other once more.

The skies sang, the ocean roared with laughter and the sun caressed her dear children, knowing that the time had come for all to become magic once more.

These two gazed into each other's eyes with sheer delight, for they knew their real journey of magic had just begun . . .

There was once mentioned a great secret. This secret was the moment when the two became one once more.

This was the tale of the courage of all the ages, when the wisdom of the head sought the wisdom of the heart and surrendered.

The greatest shock was in the understanding that in surrendering to the wisdom of the heart, the heart had surrendered to the wisdom of the head ... and then the greatest alchemy of all time was born.

He and she created the immortality of grace.

So be it!

# What is Mine?

*Mine is the ocean, the skies overhead,
The laughter, the elements, all that I tread;
The finest of homes and the wildest of fields,
The harvest I reap and the joy that I feel.*

*Mine is the love that I see in all things,
The eyes that see all and the voice that does sing;
The castles of old upon mountains so high,
The moon as it rises amongst darkened skies.*

*The treasures so great that are buried so deep,
Of ancient ones told, of language we keep;
Mine is the darkness in beauty so bright,
As mysteries open, as stories heed sight.*

*Mine are the chivalrous stories of old,
The greatest of loves and the coldest of foes;
The ever increasing knowledge of why,
And all that I capture as I perceive why.*

*Mine is the notion that spreads through me now,
Of life's fullest meaning, of so many hows;
Of all that I know to be purpose so true,
Of love that I witness in truth that is you.*

*That is mine.*

*More about
'The Ahqulieah Chronicles;
The Flight of the Eagle',
the author,
and some of the
characters within
the book*

'The Ahqulieah Chronicles;
The Flight of the Eagle'
is, like 'The Sacred Quest' book
before it, based entirely upon
the true experience of the author.

Many of the characters within the book
appear in their true identity;
some have chosen not to.

# About the Author

## Author Biography:

## Louise Ahqulieah Langley

As she followed her intuition implicitly after a meeting with a mysterious stranger in Dublin two and a half years ago, a journey unfolded about Louise, one which has had both her and all around her astounded.

What was this journey?

One that was to understand and embrace the truth of the amazing journey of life, the Sacred Union of the self. One which was to bring great truths across time and space to the fore, one which had her reeling as she began to understand why so many people across the notion of time had presented their truth, their sacred truth, no matter what the cost to them would be.

One which became her Sacred Quest.

Why? Because, for the first time in her life, she trusted her heart, her intuition implicitly and without hesitation.

From that moment in Dublin, following her heart took the greatest courage. A huge paradigm shift saw her walk away from an extremely successful career in high value financial sales and from a marriage.

To the amazement of those around her who really didn't understand what was happening to her at the time, she flouted all society's conditioning to follow her heart, knowing it to hold the only truth that mattered.

As she did so, she began to understand how to love the journey, knowing it to be a game, a story she had laid out for herself to follow . . . when the moment for her to remember was apparent.

Now, Louise is an international speaker, having travelled from Australia to Antarctica speaking across the world. She is the author of her first, world renowned and loved book 'The Sacred Quest'.

Louise gives workshop retreats, continues to appear in television and film around the globe and teaches others her inspirational message to live solely by their intuition.

## A Message from Louise

How am I so sure that, by following your heart, your intuition, that you will discover your own amazing story, your sacred purpose, your sacred truth?

I would like to share with you a magical journey, a quest to uncover your sacred truth.

"What is truth?" I hear you ask. Indeed, what is the truth?

Could it be possible that the truth were something so extraordinary, so exquisite that, once you found it, touched it, your life would quite literally transform before your eyes?

Could it be that the trail to discover this truth, a truth withheld from you across the ages, were merely a trail that you had left for you to find in 'the perfect moment?'

What if 'the perfect moment' has arrived?

Now . . .

In the summer of 2006, the perfect moment was upon me. I had no idea that I was about to touch the sacred truth. As I stood on a Dublin street, in the early hours of a long night, suspended in the midst of the mist that clung to every beautiful moment that unfolded about me, the sacred truth began to be revealed.

I was staggered, wretched and yet touched in that moment by something so exquisite that the moments before that point in my life quite literally disappeared. I had no idea that the sacred truth could be so extraordinarily beautiful. I had no idea that I could possibly be worthy of this sacred truth I was witnessing. And yet, with all my soul I yearned for this to be the truth, as much as I knew with all my soul that I had just touched the truth.

Where did I go from here?

I knew then that the pursuit of the truth in totality was the only path I could possibly pursue. I had no idea where to begin as I returned to England, withdrawing from everyone and everything.

Until, I began to understand that my navigational steer was something so profound and yet so simple!

As I followed this implicitly, without question or hesitation, the most extraordinary journey began to unfold about me. This journey has taught me that one thing above all is the only basis upon which to experience life. That is to always, implicitly, and without hesitation, trust and follow your intuition, your heart, your inner guidance.

In so doing, a trail of synchronicities and synergies unfolding about you and incredible knowledge from within sets out an amazing trail for you to follow. This trail quite literally becomes the journey you laid out for you to complete.

You have just arrived at one point in your journey, consciously or not, where you determined to discover The Sacred Truth.

You have the right to understand now that life is an amazing game. You have the right to know that inspiration is your dearest friend and guide and that the only truth is the truth within you.

What liberation to know that you are quite literally the creator of your own journey and that the journey is always perfect.

I invite you now to come with me on a journey of discovery, a journey which will provide you with a glimpse of The Sacred Truth, the truth you always intended for you to find . . . in the perfect moment.

The perfect moment that would see you unfold your sacred purpose.

Please visit www.louiselangley.com and register for free to receive The Sacred Truth mini-course.

*About some of the Characters within 'The Ahqulieah Chronicles; The Flight of the Eagle'*

*A message from Lee, as featured within The Ahqulieah Chronicles*

## Alchemy

"The mind can understand the literal meaning of the word alchemy in a few seconds, but the soul understands the meaning only when you are ready.

Enjoy your journey, wishing you magic . . ."

Lee

To contact Lee for a clairvoyant psychic telephone reading, telephone UK 0800 1216820 or 0845 6070207

*A message from Cherry,
as featured within
The Ahqulieah Chronicles*

## Uncovering Magical Secrets from your Past

"Regression to the Soul and past lives awakens long forgotten knowledge and sheds a light that enables us to walk this life with greater ease, understanding and clarity."

Cherry


To contact Cherry for a past life regression or healing visit: www.emeryesoterics.co.uk

## A message from Emma, editor of The Ahqulieah Chronicles

### Who are you really?

"The journey of self-discovery requires you to gently peel back the layers and let go of all that you thought you were. There is no better gift you can give to yourself, than finding the 'real' you."

Emma

In addition to editorial services, Emma also offers Soul and Past Life Coaching and an in depth 28 Day Programme. For more information, please visit her website www.time2beme.co.uk.

*Life is a journey of unfolding miracles.*

*Explore more with Louise at
www.louiselangley.com*

# What happens when you dare to follow your heart?

A meeting with a mysterious stranger propels a young woman onto a magical journey; a trail which she comes to realise has been left for her to follow.

# The Sacred Quest Music CD and Audio Book

A stunning compilation of music created by a talented young musician, Matt Emery.

Matt wrote this music specifically for The Sacred Quest Audio book, which is narrated by the author.

Both are available to purchase from www.louiselangley.com

## The Sacred Life Path

*"Are you ready to fully experience your divine nature by stepping onto your Sacred Life Path?"*

*Workshop Retreats with Louise, details at www.louiselangley.com*

### Here's what you'll learn...

- ✓ How to recognise and uncover your own Sacred Quest and continue on the path no matter how crazy it seems.

- ✓ How to connect with and then follow your intuition implicitly, utterly and without question.

- ✓ How to honour and trust the most amazing and sacred truth in existence and tap into Sacred Powers that will enable you to manifest all that your heart truly wants.

- ✓ How to start fully living your life once and for all right now!